Marjorie Graham was born in Edinburgh in 1904 and lived a rich, varied life until her death in 1974.

Clive Murphy was born in Liverpool in 1935. He has devoted much of the past forty years to recording, editing and publishing his 'Ordinary Lives' series of autobiographies, saving the memoirs of an extensive range of urban and rural characters for posterity. He lives in Spitalfields.

The 'Ordinary Lives' series, recorded
and edited by Clive Murphy

The Good Deeds of a Good Woman:
The Memoirs of an East End Hostel-Dweller
BEATRICE ALI

Born to Sing: The Memoirs of
an East End Mantle Presser
ALEXANDER HARTOG

Four Acres and a Donkey:
The Memoirs of a Lavatory Attendant
S. A. B. ROGERS

Up in Lights (originally published as Love, Dears!):
The Memoirs of a former Chorus Girl
MARJORIE GRAHAM

Oiky: The Memoirs of a Pigman
LEN MILLS

At the Dog in Dulwich: The Memoirs of a Poet
PATRICIA DOUBELL

A Stranger in Gloucester: The Memoirs of
an Austrian in England
MRS FALGE-WAHL

A Funny Old Quist: The Memoirs of a Gamekeeper
EVAN ROGERS

Dodo: The Memoirs of a Left-Wing Socialite
DODO LEES

Endsleigh: The Memoirs of a River-Keeper
HORACE ADAMS

Up in Lights

The Memoirs of a 1920s Chorus Girl

MARJORIE GRAHAM

recorded and edited by
Clive Murphy

PAN BOOKS

First published 1980 by Dobson Books Ltd, London

This edition first published in paperback 2013 by Pan Books
an imprint of Pan Macmillan, a division of Macmillan Publishers Limited
Pan Macmillan, 20 New Wharf Road, London N1 9RR
Basingstoke and Oxford
Associated companies throughout the world
www.panmacmillan.com

ISBN 978-1-4472-4388-5

Photograph on previous page: Miss Graham in
The Sleeping Beauty, 1928, courtesy of the author.

Originally published in 1980 as *Love, Dears!*
book four in the 'Ordinary Lives' series, recorded and edited by Clive Murphy.

1 3 5 7 9 8 6 4 2

A CIP catalogue record for this book is available from
the British Library.

Typeset by Ellipsis Digital Limited, Glasgow
Printed by CPI Group (UK) Ltd, Croydon, CR0 4YY

Visit **www.panmacmillan.com** to read more about all our books
and to buy them. You will also find features, author interviews and
news of any author events, and you can sign up for e-newsletters
so that you're always first to hear about our new releases.

*I dedicate this book to
my darling Mumsie*

CHAPTER ONE

I lived at 304, Morningside Road, Edinburgh, till 1910 when I was six but, apart from Daddy carrying me up the stone stairs from my pram to our fifth floor flat, and Mother leaving me across the car-lines to go to Miss Hunter's Private School, I can't remember much about my infancy save being dressed up in skins with a girl called Lily Roberts to raise funds for Donaldson's Hospital.

It was swelteringly hot and the skins didn't help. At three o'clock in the afternoon, with sweat pouring down our faces, we danced 'The Teddy Bears' Picnic'. Mother said, 'Well done!

You won't have to dance again till five, so you can get out of those skins and have an ice-cream.' That suited us fine. We got our ice-creams and cooled off and sat under the trees. When it was time to get back into the skins, I said to Lily, 'We're going to have another ice-cream.' She said, 'We've had our ice-cream.' I said, 'We'll get another.' She said, 'How?' I said, 'Wait and see!'

My mother came up full of how everyone was saying how marvellous we little kids were performing on this hot afternoon and how young we were to be so good. 'Come on now, girlies!' she said. 'You've had your rest. Time to get ready. Into your skins! I know they're not very nice, but you've only one dance to do and then we're off home.' Cocky-bit sits up and says, 'Could we have another ice-cream, please?' 'Oh no, darling! You don't want to have another ice-cream just before dancing. You've *had* an ice-cream. You've cooled down. You'll get one when you're finished.' 'No,' I said, 'we'll have one now or we won't dance!' 'Marjorie! You naughty girl! How *dare* you say that!' She got really angry. 'If you don't go on I'll give you a whipping!' I was determined. Before she could make me go on, we got our ice-creams. Blackmail – at four years old!

We moved to Alloa, Clackmannanshire, the smallest county in Scotland. That was where Daddy went all wrong with drink. Alloa had eight breweries. No-one went shopping on a Friday, the smell was so obnoxious. He was an accountant at Calder's, a firm of brewers in opposition to Younger's. He was a wizard. He could add four rows of figures in a wink. But he needed his whisky. 'Has Daddy got his whisky?' was like 'Has Daddy got his slippers?' He had a tantalus – three big bottles in a cabinet, each one filled with whisky. I never thought it odd. I told my friends, 'Daddy always has to have his whisky!' and Mumsie said, 'Oh, you mustn't say that!'

Daddy didn't spoil my childhood. He only spoiled me. He left it to my mother to try to mould my character. When she asked him to whip me, he wouldn't and I knew he wouldn't. She could never threaten me by saying, 'When Daddy comes home, *he'll* do something!' I shall never forget her taking her hand to me. I cried and cried and cried. Not because she hurt me, but because the tears were pouring down her face. She never whipped me again.

Daddy seemed delightful. He bought me an upright piano and paid a Miss Cock to give me lessons. He painted wild seascapes in oils in the kick-in room where I kept my bicycle. Tears ran down his face when I played or sang. He cried a lot. He cried at the theatre. Mother used to say, 'Norman! Please don't let people see you! It looks awful to see a man with tears on his face! Use this handkerchief!' He drew cartoons. There was one of me sitting at the piano, an enormous ribbon and a wee skinty plait over a broad back and bottom. Unlike my mother, he never went to church. He said he'd read the Bible from cover to cover and could pray anywhere. He wrote plays for me and my friends. Mother gave us cocoa and buns, and he directed. I bossed. My best friend to begin with was May Small. She had to do some heavy acting. She tried to cry at rehearsals and couldn't. I got so worked up, I dashed at her and shook her and smacked her face. I couldn't understand why she wouldn't *give* anything.

I had acting in the blood. Before we left the Academy at home time the teacher would say, 'Now Marjorie's going to sing to you. All sit round in a ring.' So I stood in the middle and sang 'The Petticoat Song' from *Miss Hook of Holland* which my Auntie Day taught me when she came to visit. Auntie Day was on the stage in London. She had funny eyes. One was brown, the other a mixture of brown and green. Her hair was dyed red. Instead of a hat she wore a chiffon bandeau. People looked round at her in the street. I thought everything she said and did was right. She was more attractive to me than my own mother.

Mother had sad, grey-blue eyes, a Cupid's bow and high cheekbones. Her nose was big for a woman's, rather like an Indian's. Her hair was reddy-chestnut, tidily done on top, usually with a small becoming hat – but she hadn't enough to make coils. She was very slim. I don't take after her in that way at all. As a matter of fact I don't take after her in any way whatever, which used to upset her considerably. When people said, 'Your daughter isn't a bit like you!', she said, 'Don't you

5

think a *little* bit?' She had a lovely smile and she never lost her temper. Her weakest feature was her neck. Daddy and I used to tease her: 'You've got a swanlike neck!' 'Don't you believe it!' she'd say. 'I've a scraggy neck which I hate, and I've no bust either!' She'd neat feet and ankles, and good legs – but in those days you didn't show your legs; you even played tennis in long skirts. Her hands were well shaped, despite blacking grates and scrubbing floors as the eldest daughter of a large family. She was a first-class dressmaker and dressed herself beautifully. I can always remember a costume she wore one Visiting Day: a royal blue coat in a warm woolly material, very tightly fitted, with a black astrakhan high neck and black astrakhan cuffs. A black astrakhan hat went with it, and black lacing shoes and black silk stockings. 'But what does your father look like?' the children asked. 'Handsome,' I said, 'but he doesn't like coming to school.' Daddy didn't like going out anywhere, except to drink at a hotel. Once, he came to see me swim at Alloa Baths and I won a silver cup presented by Sir John Paton of Paton's Wools. He was so happy and excited! He said, 'I never thought my nipper could do it.'

In those days I got everything I wanted by foul means or fair. Mother gave strict instructions before visiting Mrs Bowie next door. 'Marjorie, when Mrs Bowie asks you to have a cake, you accept and finish. If she asks you again, unless she presses you, you refuse.' I go to tea, am asked to have a cake. I accept and thoroughly enjoy it. Mrs Bowie brings the cake tray round again and says, 'Have another cake, Marjorie.' I answer, 'No thank you, Mrs Bowie, but Mumsie says if you press me I would like one, please.'

We were in mixed classes at Alloa Academy from the age of seven. The boys were on one side, the girls on the other. I always managed to get near the boys. There was a special boy Barney Waller, nice looking, rather shy. To get near me, he used to say to the teacher, 'Please, Miss, I can't hear you properly. Can I move to the bench in front?' There we sat, he at the end of his bench, me at the end of mine, with a corridor down the middle and our little desks carved with hearts and arrows and 'I love you's' in front of us. Oh, how I loved Barney! There was another boy called Ramsey Stewart. He was a real Scot, red-faced and always in the kilt. I couldn't bear him, but I had to put up with him because he was Barney's pal.

I met Barney after school one day shopping in the town. He said, 'I've got some cream buns. Will you come back home? Mother's out, so we can eat them in the kitchen.' We got home. We had our cream buns in the kitchen and Barney asked would I like to see his Cub Medals in the bedroom. We had little cuddles and fights on the bed and thought we were wonderful.

I don't believe children should be told about sex till they come to the age of puberty. Why not be allowed to find out with the same sensations as an animal finds out? Too much knowledge kills their natural human instinct to want to have contact. When I was ten I was asked by a girl of the same age did I know how babies were made. I said, 'No, how *are* they made?' She said, 'A boy does a dribble in a pot and you do a dribble too.' What a damned, ridiculous, silly thing, but it's better than 'This goes in here,' and

'A baby comes out there,' before the poor little souls are ready.

At puberty my mother told me not to worry if I woke up bleeding; this was something that happened to every girl. She told me nothing about boys, and I never was sure *exactly* what men had or hadn't until I met my first lover. I hadn't even seen naked boys because at the swimming baths they always wore trews. Nor can I say I was thrilled when eventually I *did* find out. I was very glad I was a woman. I thought, 'Your figure is quite as attractive as mine, but I don't like the gadgets.' That was until I'd had some usage of them.

I gave up May Small for a ginger girl with freckles called Edith. She was allowed to drabble on the streets till all hours and I was intrigued that she could love someone one minute and hate them the next. At school if she was asked to draw a vase she'd draw a woman in a gown. She said, 'I can't draw a vase, so I've drawn a woman in a gown.' At twelve years old she put on a Blue-beard Tableau. I was the one wife that escaped. She designed her own trousers and papier mâché sword. For a set she had a white sheet with real girls' heads sticking out, chalk white with blood on their necks and on the sheet. She went on to become a glamorous model in London. Though plain in the face, she grew tall and graceful, with her hair drawn back to a bun low down. With the help of makeup she was able to lose her freckles. It was she who started the craze of wearing only one earring.

Edith was in Higher Grade. So was Jim Cuthbert. Jim and I became sweethearts. He was fair with blue eyes. He danced. He swam. He was an athlete. My mother and father accepted him at the house because his father was a solicitor. He was the first boy to give me a lover's kiss. We were playing a version of Postman's Knock. Jim knocked at the door and called for me to go outside. What a thrill!

During the First World War, he went away to HMS Peyton as a midshipman. He wrote to me religiously and Mother suggested I knit him a pair of socks. I couldn't bear knitting, but she offered to cast them on. He got them months later. I had to keep telling him they were on their way. 'I don't know that he'll ever wear these, darling,' said Mother when I finished them at last. 'I think they'll hurt his toes.'

Chapter Two

addy, who loved me to death and, if he had kept his reason, would have made a mess of me, proposed either that I 'finish' at Dollar Academy, which was ten minutes from Alloa in the train, or that I come to London where a thousand-a-year accountant's job was waiting for him with MacDougall's, the timber merchants. He gave me the choice, so of course I said, 'I don't want to go to any Dollar Finishing School! I want to be a film star!'

On Armistice Night, 1918, my aunt, who belonged to the Chelsea set and went everywhere and knew everyone, got Mother and me tickets for an all-round show at the Palladium. We went on a bus but we couldn't get any conveyance home. There was noise. There was lights-up. There were taxis passing with people sitting on the luggage rails and dangling their legs and shouting and waving flags. It took us a couple of hours to get from Oxford Street to Pimlico. We had to walk one behind the other with little steps. People were drunk. Mother was worried at having me out amongst such a crowd. But it wasn't a crowd you'd be hurt in. It was a slow-moving crowd which didn't care when it got home. It didn't shove and push like those awful crowds you get at football matches. People were so happy. They were so full of joy. Everybody loved everybody else.

Daddy was still up North. We had taken a furnished flat in Claverton Street. Suddenly, he wrote to say that he'd sold the furniture, including my piano, because we wouldn't need it. He'd sold *my* piano that he'd bought and given to me. I never forgave him. It was nobody's but mine.

Now at that age you get something done to you and you never forget it. Right till Daddy died

I resented that one thing he did. I felt, 'What a horrible thing to do!' I feel it to this day. It isn't a thing I'd do to anybody. He gave me a present. He said, 'I love you. You're my daughter. I give you this. I've worked for it and I've paid for it.' Then, just when I was interested in getting on and when I wanted to use it to learn songs and practise them and play them for myself, he wrote with the news, 'You've no piano. I've sold it'. When for two years he drank and drank and drank and hardly ate at all, I didn't care. When he lost his job, I didn't care. When, in the bedroom, he shouted, 'I'm going to tear the sheet from one end to the other, rip it to pieces!', I said, 'That's silly. It's too easy. I could do that. Why not tear something really difficult?' and I picked up a mat and gave it to him.

At last we got him incarcerated somewhere in Kilburn. He couldn't read. He couldn't remember. He could only count very slowly, like a child. He went from home to home, and I visited him because it was my duty. He lived to eighty-three. When I got notice of his death in The Lady Something Home in Streatham, I felt no love. I didn't want to see him in the mortuary. I took a sheaf of flowers to the door.

The Elephant and Castle staged a big pantomime every Christmas. I changed my name from Marjorie Hunter to Marjorie Graham, and went for an audition. I did a little dance. I'd only done ballroom dancing at school, so I improvised. I copied Jessie Matthews. I danced for five minutes. The director, a fatherly man with greying temples, called, 'That's enough, thank you! Go to the side. I might want you back.' Well, he did call me back, and I had to sing him a number in my tiny tuneful voice, and he engaged me. I wanted to kiss him. My first job! Two pounds a week and only a twopenny bus-ride home!

I was supposed to be a Chinese coolie. When it came to the dress rehearsal they issued out the coolie clothes. I was given a tiger skin, sandals and a big straw coolie hat. I went away, made my face into a dark dirty yellow, dressed, and sailed downstairs and on to the stage, thinking I looked marvellous. The director's mouth opened. His eyes popped. He said, 'My God! What the hell have you done with your face?' 'I'm a coolie,' I said. 'Maybe,' he said, 'but in pantomime we don't make up coolies to look like coolies. You go back and make your face what it is. It's a very pretty face.' It took me years to understand what he meant.

We ran nine to ten weeks. I thought I was on the way. I wrote to Elstree and was offered a screen test. I'd to act a sort of Queen of the East with a bosom – covered in draperies, of course. In those days *everything* had to be covered, which was just as well, considering my waistline. I went home to Mother conceitedly satisfied. Though I was just a baby in face of so many beautiful and experienced people seeking employment, I thought there was some hope.

I was put on the crowd list. In all I must have appeared in twenty films but I have never been able to find myself. You took the workmen's train to Elstree and got the fare and a pound in your hand at the end of the day. You were sent a letter in advance telling you what to wear. You were expected to have day clothes for walking in the street, and evening clothes for receptions and scenes in restaurants – anything else, such as period costume, was supplied and fitted by Wardrobe. Because of Daddy's drinking, Mother had taken up dressmaking in a big way, so she was able to help me. I sometimes saw Gracie Fields' second husband directing. He wore a French beret and a dirty long moustache, and shouted. In the restaurant he ate spaghetti in a disgusting manner with two forks up in the air.

My love life wasn't running smoothly. At the Ham and Bone Club behind Piccadilly I had met Freke Fairwell, a captain in the Royal Engineers. He was tall and handsome with a little moustache and ruddy cheeks. There was a fresh country look about him, and he danced beautifully. But he wouldn't introduce me to his people. 'My dear,' he said, 'my family are very narrow. I'm afraid they mightn't like your being on the stage.' That hurt my pride.

I longed to join the tour of *Joy Bells*, a revue which was running successfully at the Hippodrome with George Robey in the lead. Gus Solke, the dancer and producer, auditioned me. I wore a short skirt pleated in navy blue with a tight pair of pants, bare legs, white socks and black dancing shoes. My hair was in a page-boy bob, turned under. Gus Solke was a repulsive little man, the size of tuppence. I've never seen anyone so ugly. He looked as though someone had stood on his face. He might have been a boxer. But he could dance! He just wafted over the floor. Feet and body, he was like a rubber ball.

I was about twentieth. I was a bundle of shattered nerves. I had prepared a piece to sing which he didn't want. In very broken English he said, 'Now, my dear, I vant you to do like-a thees. It von't be good first time. Vatch me. Not be scare.' My heart sank. I felt sick. He danced along the stage while I watched, and then I did the same or, rather, as near as I could copy. He said, 'Good.' Whew! Gracious me. From *him*! 'Just vait on the side.'

It was a big chorus of dancers he wanted. He went through another and another and another and I still waited on the side. Then I was engaged, so young and on my own merits and just by copying. I suppose Solke knew that you just have dancing feet or you haven't. I'd had no training except the occasional half-a-crown lesson with the Tiller Troupe. Plain old grumpy Mrs Tiller would sit with her stick watching the teacher and if she saw a leg out of rhythm she whacked it as it passed. One look at my waist and she said, 'Skip an extra hour each day, and forget to eat cream buns for tea!'

I went straight on tour. We played Edinburgh, Glasgow, Leeds, Bradford, Sheffield – all the Number One towns. Gladys Lloyd, later Lady Cobham, was the female lead. Ernest Sefton, brother of Violet Lorraine, took George Robey's part. Mother told me while on tour to put a hand-mirror over the sheets to see if they were damp.

Next came a Number One tour of *The Maid of the Mountains* – front row chorus. When we arrived in Belfast everything looked like war. There were tanks diving down the streets and we had to give performances an hour earlier than expected because of a curfew. On the third night, before the interval and in the middle of a big number, a shot was fired among the audience. There was uproar. The house lights went up, and we on the stage were cut off by the curtain.

Finish. We were told to go to our dressing-rooms, then leave the theatre.

In 1922 *Sybil* opened at the Prince's, Manchester, with José Collins and Harry Welchman. I was in the chorus as a singer, a sweet five foot three in flat heels. With me was Stella O'Neill from Donegal, beautiful, with curly red hair and a fair complexion. José Collins had an awful temper and was so powerful she could have you sacked in a minute. In one scene, as Sybil impersonating the Grand Duchess Anna Pavlovna, she had to walk down the centre of the stage, all in sequins and holding an enormous white ostrich-feather fan. The fan covered her entire body with the exception of her face, and sometimes she even hid her face so she could talk as she passed the lines of chorus girls on either side, standing poised and looking nice. One night as she was passing Stella and me she said, 'Your figure is hell!' We let out 'Bitch!' simultaneously, neither of us knowing which one she referred to, though Stella's figure *was* hell so I'd a good idea. Stella was sent for afterwards. She came up again in tears. 'She wiped the floor with me! She said, "Stand so as not to look pregnant even if you are!"'

Once *I* was sent for. I thought, 'Oh Lord, what the hell have I been doing? I bet she's caught me talking again on stage.' But when I entered her dressing-room she said, 'Hello!' with a marvellous smile, 'Could you use that?' and flung me a beautiful black silk cocktail dress that couldn't have been on her back twice.

Seymour Hicks, who produced the show, was a devil. To get back to London with the big noises, rather than go on tour from town to town, you had to sleep with him. I couldn't for a while believe it; his wife, Ellaline Terriss, was the most beautiful woman in the world. Then he came to me as bold as brass. 'How about supper tonight and a little love afterwards?' I was so taken aback I nearly said Yes. Instead, I went on tour again. There was a chorus boy who carried my luggage and bought me lunch. He wasn't for keeps. He was just a lost soul, a married man in need of a little bit of love. Stella came too. I was so fond of her that, when we got off the night train somewhere on a Sunday, I went to Mass with her and lit candles without having had a cup of tea.

Chapter Three

Between engagements there were three ways in which I 'rested' – as a film extra hanging around Elstree; as a soubrette singing 'The Dear Little Garden I Love' and 'Song of the Homeland' at Masonic dinners; and as a waitress in the City. I worked as a waitress in a café by the Stock Exchange. Angel Court was the address. It was all very simple. Coffee, tea, sandwiches. Red lamps on the tables. Tablecloths one day pink, another blue. I was given a short-fitting black silk frock, black stockings, high-heeled black shoes, a white muslin apron and a silver tray – just like a stage maid – and there I was being nice to men from the Stock Exchange coming in to place bets with the manageress, a hard Scotswoman seated at a desk in one corner.

At Angel Court I met every type. Squareface Goldberg took me to his box at the Chelsea Arts Ball. He went as Beau Brummel – grey topper, tight-fitting grey trousers, grey tails and a stunning white cravat. I wore a Turkish harem costume with a multi-coloured veil and a sleeveless knee-length coat over baggy trousers and sandals. During some dances the huge crystal chandelier was fully lit, during others all was darkness save for spotlights following chosen couples. Though I went back with him to breakfast at his Knightsbridge home, Squareface was no more than a dear friend without sex appeal. I loved him like a father. He took me to the Café Royal and to Simpson's.

Tony Reid, another 'client', was altogether nastier. Strange how young girls when they first become sexy often fall for an older man. After dinner at the Trocadero – or was it the Savoy? – I vaguely remember going back to his flat in Lancaster Gate. I must have been a little drunk. The lights were low, and, as I came to my senses, I was aware of being on a bed and something pushing up inside me and causing me pain.

I ran and ran in floods of tears till I caught a taxi where I squealed all the way home like a little pig. Mother was asleep. Controlling myself, I crept miserably into my divan. Oh how Tony Reid disgusted me! I hated men because of him. I assumed they were all the same.

But no, they weren't. In one day walked a darling man – morning coat and topper, about forty-five, Neil Fielding by name, a stockbroker, married, with a son. With Neil nothing happened for a long, long time. He only kissed me when he said goodnight. He asked to meet my mother. He took us to *The Desert Song*. I fell in love with him.

Happiness, like its opposite, often comes all at once and in plenty. In a hall in a Soho back street, I was chosen by Mr Ernest Crampton to sing in his summer Concert Party, 'Cigarettes'. Seven of us were signed: Leonard de Renzi, the baritone, to sing duets with me and be stage manager; Whitwell Firth for dramatic monologues; George Barker, pianist, and his wife, Jean Harley, operatic contralto; Claude Hulbert, comedian, with Enid Trevor, comedienne. An old nanny dressed the show and did the basketing. We toured the resorts – Worthing, Bognor, Ilfracombe – from April to October. It was all very simple and I adored it. We had one spotlight, sometimes no footlights. At the Sparrow's Nest, Lowestoft, we had just one dressing-room with a partition, and, to wash, a bowlful of water from a jug.

Each of my feature songs in 'Cigarettes' required special scenery and costumes. For 'Lack-a-Day' I wore a Spanish-type dress – gold lace with large green panels over a hoop. I waved a handkerchief and did a minuetty sort of dance in between the verses. For 'Cobwebs' I wore a pink old-world dress against a background of shining cobwebs. The refrain went:

> Cobwebs, silver cobwebs,
> Now are hanging everywhere
> In the grey gloom of that old room,
> Once so dainty, so fresh and so fair;
> But the cobwebs that have gathered
> Thro' the years we've been apart

Soon would vanish, if love could banish
All the cobwebs from your heart –
Soon would vanish, if love could banish
All the cobwebs from your heart.

We got wonderful notices. Enid, though she was so lovely, played cockney skivvies with her hair all down her face. She only looked nice in a Grecian sketch with Claude called 'Cupid and Psyche'. She had to be graceful while he went madly acrobatic. When Claude came on stage, he always looked as if someone was about to creep up behind him and hit him on the head. This frightened way of his was what Ernest Crampton worked on. Claude really *was* scared, but he got away with it and by the end of the tour could calculate his laughs. He called me 'Pudding'. Years later after he and Enid married, and I was announced at the wedding reception of their daughter, they both threw their arms out and yelled 'Pudding! *Darling*!' and all the guests applauded. He was inclined during 'Cigarettes' to wander off and follow fire-engines to fires. If he was late for a meal or for rehearsal he'd excuse himself by explaining 'I took a bus to see a fire.' Mrs Trevor, when we got back to town, used to invite me to the rugger teas she gave at Rodneystone, Richmond, for Claude and Enid and Enid's five sisters with their footballer boyfriends. She looked so pretty with her blue eyes and snow-white hair at the head of the table laid with china and scones and sandwiches and home-made pastries.

But tragedy was near. One evening, after we had dined at the Ritz, Neil Fielding took me to his flat in Bloomsbury. We lay down before the roaring fire and made passionate love. It was I who suggested we go into the bedroom. Within a month I knew the worst.

Neil was wonderful. He offered to marry me after getting a divorce. I chose not to ruin his home or my own career. Mother and he talked and talked and talked. He knew someone at his club who could arrange an abortion in a private nursing home for three hundred pounds. Mother said to me, 'You know best. You have a choice. You can either marry Neil or do this.' I opted for the abortion.

I still think I decided wrongly. I should have had the baby and worked for it even if I didn't marry. I feel now that I committed murder. I have never forgiven myself. I find it hard to take that skeleton out of the cupboard and look it in the face. I have never had a baby. Not that I wanted one, if having a normal baby is what I suffered then. I woke in agony. I wasn't given a drug to send me back to sleep. All I had was Neil and Mumsie to hold my hand.

Neil paid the fares for Mother and me to take a holiday in Czechoslovakia. I'd a friend in Marienbad, Zet Arnost, who had opened a hotel there called the Casino. I wrote and asked if, in return for, say, two shows a day, whatever he wanted, at a small salary, he could offer a suite of rooms. Contracts were exchanged.

We were three months at the Casino. I was accompanied by a three-piece band – piano, violin and cello. I wore a silver-sequinned frock and a black silver-lined cloak. I sang 'Old Man River' and 'The Song Is Ended' at the tea dance and during dinner.

A young assistant manager who couldn't speak

a word of English used to walk with me for miles through the fir groves of the forest. The moonlit nights were just like day. As we walked over the pine needles there was the sissing noise of the tiny breeze. But I didn't want to make love. I still felt bad inside. He wanted to marry me. When I returned home he wrote and said so in pidgin English. Again I said No. I was still depressed. I have to admit, though, that the injury of my abortion made me stop to think. It taught me to listen to other people's troubles. If it had never happened I might have become a more horrible person than I am.

In 1925, the same year, I appeared in *Derby Day*, a musical romance by Arthur Roseberry. I played Maggie Carter to young Fred Peisley's Reggie Turner. It was my first experience of acting rather than revue, of a small musical rather than a big one. We did a Number Two tour to such places as Putney, Fulham, Golders Green, Torquay and Nuneaton. Mother made me a frock for the Equestrian Club scene. Attached to it was a long scarf I could throw back over the shoulders and use in all sorts of graceful manners.

Freddie was most odd during rehearsals. We'd be practising our lines together when suddenly he'd throw up his script and say, 'I can't do this! It's a rotten part!' During the tour, Mother came to see me in my digs and Freddie came along to supper. Suddenly Freddie rose from his chair, picked up the carving knife and went as if to cut my throat. I pretended to take it as a joke, but the next day I said to him, 'You stupid little boy, behaving like that in front of an elderly person!' He said, 'You know I've always been in love with you!'

Years later, I was sitting on top of a bus going up Regent Street when who should sit beside me but Frederick Peisley. He had done quite well, played many leading roles. I mentioned the carving knife. He said, 'Oh, didn't I behave like a fool! I've done so much dramatic acting since, it's taken all the nonsense out of me!'

My next show was *The Naughty Rajah With Diamond Eyes*, a revue directed by Fat Peterson in which I understudied Nita Croft and sang and danced a couple of numbers with chorus backing in order to relieve her.

Fat Peterson was vulgar and revolting. During

rehearsals we had gone through a number called 'The Black Bottom' once, twice, three times, and he still wasn't pleased. 'Do move your bottoms!' he shouted. We tried again. 'You there!' he yelled, pointing his finger right at me. 'Can't you wiggle your bum?!' I could have spat in his eye.

There was a Welsh girl in the chorus I didn't like at all. Once she picked up a chair and slung it at me across the chorus room with all her strength. 'You bloody Scot!' she screamed. 'You're always interfering! I hate the damned sight of you!' 'Well if you're Welsh,' I screamed in reply, 'I hope they're not all like you, you horrible beast!' The whole twenty of us in the chorus disliked her, and if twenty people disliked her there must have been *something* wrong. The first person in the chorus room on Monday morning always got the place with the best light and the best mirror for make-up. That was accepted. But she made a point of getting there every time. It got under our skin. It wasn't good sportsmanship. One other thing – she bribed the dresser to get priority treatment so she would never be late, so she would never have to hurry.

I had an extraordinary experience while we were doing a one-week stand in Eccles. A plain-clothes detective came round from front of house and said, 'Is your name Miss Marjorie Graham?' 'That's right,' I said. 'What on earth do you want?' 'Is this your photograph?' he said. 'I have reason to believe it is, and that you left two of a family behind you after your last date.' I looked at the photo. It *was* very like me. 'But I'm not married!' I explained. 'That's your story!' he said. 'Aren't you really a mother who has abandoned her children of two and three?'

He refused to let me leave till I gave him some proof I was not the woman he was looking for, so I had to spend the night in that theatre! Nita stayed with me. She demanded it. We slept fully clothed on benches in the manager's office with a blanket over us, *locked in*!

In the morning the police sent in coffee and hot rolls. An hour later, the detective appeared. 'I'm very sorry,' he said. 'The girl we're looking for has been picked up two stations down the line.'

CHAPTER FOUR

P antomime, not revue, was to be the last, as well as the first, of my encounters with the theatre. In 1927, Blanche Littler, sister of the Littler brothers and eventually George Robey's wife, was managing the Artillery Theatre, Woolwich, on her own. Nita and I agreed to play for her in *Aladdin*. Nita was Aladdin and I was Princess Balroubadour. In other words, we were Principal Boy and Girl.

Nita was a success, but there were certain criticisms. For instance, I was eleven stone and seemed to get heavier every night. Four chorus boys had to carry me in reclining on a palanquin.

'Come on, boys!' 'Get your muscles up!' 'Here we go again!' – they used to make jokes like that at every performance. Once they dropped the palanquin upstage. It wasn't time for my cue from Nita so I simply lay there, trying to look unconcerned. Then I forgot I'd have further to walk, and was late reaching Nita who had to deliver the cue to me twice. Another night I sang one verse and one chorus and, when I opened my mouth to sing the second verse, not a sound came out. The audience applauded thinking the song was over. I'd laryngitis and had to miss a whole week. My understudy played the part and got my salary. In those days, if you were off you were off. You received no compensation.

Next year, I set my sights on something higher – Principal Boy in *The Sleeping Beauty* at the King's Theatre, Edinburgh. This appealed to me as I was born in Edinburgh, and my grandfather of eighty (Mother's side) was living with my mother's eldest brother and his wife and two boys in a flat right opposite the theatre. I wrote a personal letter to Stewart Cruickshank, then Managing Director of Howard and Wyndham's, the owners.

Mr Cruickshank offered me an audition on the stage of the Adelphi. I duly presented myself in black tights, a black fitting top – long sleeves: no naked business – and black briefs. I looked black the whole way up.

I was so eager to get the part, I arrived on time. There were about two hundred of us. I watched what the ones ahead of me had to do – walk straight down the middle with full lights on them, hand their song to the pianist, sing a few lines, and receive a 'Thank you, that will do. Now trip a little dance for me,' then 'Thank you, Miss So-and-So. Will you just wait. You'll hear before you go home.' They were 'Chorus', and I was aiming for Principal Boy. I was kidding myself.

I walked down and passed my song over to the pianist. 'The name, please?' I'd never met Mr Cruickshank, and you can't see what a man looks like over the footlights. They are usually very rude and abrupt. But Mr Cruickshank wasn't. He was nicely spoken and polite. He said, 'Thank you, Miss Graham. Will you sing your song?' I did my few lines, finished that; did my little dance, finished that. 'Thank you, Miss Graham. Will you just please wait.'

The two hundred of us waited for what seemed a hell of a time to get the usual 'Thank you very much. I'm afraid we've got all we want.'

Finally Mr Cruickshank came up onto the stage and said 'I'll call out the names of those I want back.' About six were called. I was called first. 'Miss Graham,' he said, 'I'd like to see you to arrange a three-year contract, as Second Boy for two years in Edinburgh and, if all goes well, Principal Boy in Glasgow the third. Does that suit?' I was most excited. I said, 'Oh, how lovely, Mr Cruickshank!' He said, 'Now, my dear, you live in London? . . . Well, I'm going back to Edinburgh tomorrow. Are you free to dine with me tonight?' I was taken aback, but I said, 'Certainly. Where would that be?' 'At the Mayfair. Eight o'clock? We'll sign then and fix the details.'

I sensed he liked me in a fatherly way, but Mother said, 'You haven't signed the contract and you're going to dinner at the Mayfair? How do you know it's not another Seymour Hicks?'

I was short of money yet I had to have a taxi as I was in evening dress. I said to myself, 'My God, don't let it rain! I'll catch a bus up to Hyde

Park Corner and take a taxi from there. I can't just sail into the hotel off the streets. It isn't done.' So that's what happened. I drove up to the Mayfair in a two bob taxi, having taken the bus to Hyde Park from Blandford Street where we were now living.

I met Cruickshank in the lounge, where we had cocktails. He was a charming, well-preserved sixty. The dinner went most successfully. I evidently amused him, and I had everything I wanted, including champagne. Out came the contract. 'This is too good to be true!' I thought. 'It's going to be signed before "the after of dinner"!' I said, 'Wasn't I lucky to be picked out of so many?' This was in part false modesty as I knew I was pretty and could sing and dance. He said, 'You won that Second Boy because you had the best legs.'

There were two snags. He didn't pay the fare and there would be a fortnight of rehearsals without money. Could I fill in meantime? I was still very wary. I said, 'I'll have to. Perhaps we'd better discuss it with my mother.' 'We'll do that,' he said. 'But, tell me, what do you say to twenty pounds a week for the first year and twenty-five for the second? In the third, naturally, there will be a big jump as you'll be Principal Boy.' Never before had I been offered so much!

Back to Blandford Street he took me in a taxi. No demonstrations. Nothing. Just an elderly gentleman, kind in every way. My mother made him a cup of coffee and, there and then, we signed that contract. On it, he added, 'I guarantee to pay Miss Graham's fare of £3-10 to Edinburgh.' It was the best thing that had ever happened to me in my whole life.

The Sleeping Beauty lasted the usual nine weeks. Dorée Thorne was Principal Boy, and Myrette Morven Second Girl. There was one big scene which opened with everyone asleep. Then the Fairy woke us up. I came to life in a pale pink doublet and tights; Myrette was in a full blue skirt. We all wore white wigs. Myrette and I took the centre of the stage in a Grand Minuet, with the Principal Boy and Girl at the back to make a 'picture'.

It was a happy season, and I lived with my family opposite the theatre. Ron Robertson, my cousin, was planning to go to Australia to train in agriculture as leader of twelve Scout Rovers. At present he was in a paint works, which he hated. He was eighteen and beginning to take an interest in girls so I suggested he come over to the chorus dressing-room for tea. I knew the girls would make a fuss of him as he was terribly good-looking in the kilt and Scout hat.

All was arranged. We put special cakes ready and, after the matinée, the kettle was boiling on the wire netting above the pipe. The doorman sent Ron up, and in he walked! Every one of us was in bra and knicks, either rolling or being rolled with Punkt rollers! No man was ever supposed to see you like that! Not even a chorus boy!

Ron opened his mouth, went red in the face, and turned to leave. I called 'Ron! There you are! Excuse us. Who said you could come in before we yelled?' I could see he thought he had done something dreadful and that we were doing dreadful things as well. But we all put on our kimonos and had a lovely tea, and, by the time he left, he had lost all his shyness. The girls kissed him goodbye and told him he was the handsomest boy they had ever seen.

The following year I played Captain Toprail in *Robinson Crusoe*, against Myrette Morven, and was asked to understudy Victoria Carmen, the leading lady.

Mother made me the most fabulous velvet coat for rehearsals. It was long and black, rather wide at the foot, with huge cuffs and a skunk collar. It was like something from Paris. Myrette when she first saw it said, 'My! What a whopper of a coat!' Her mother was in the stalls one day. When we broke for lunch she said, '*You*'ve come into the money!' She went to touch it. 'You know,' she said, 'sitting in the stalls I thought it was sealskin!'

Something new had happened that year in the West End – Beatrice Lillie had had the first Eton crop. Everybody was talking about it. I thought, 'I've got a lovely purple get-up for my entrance. I'll change my hair.' I said to the Fairy, 'What do you think about my having an Eton crop?' She said, 'I think it would be grand. And why not have it blonded as well for when you take off your three-cornered hat?'

Well, the company went stark staring mad and thought it was wonderful. Stewart Cruickshank had a walk down to the theatre during rehearsals to see it. He said, 'How marvellous! I'm glad you thought of that. Get into your costume. I'm going down into the stalls. Before dress rehearsal I want to see how it looks under the lights.' I made an entrance for him specially. He said, 'Oh, what an improvement on the bob! I like this *much* better! Bea Lillie has it in the West End, and now we've got it here in Edinburgh too!'

I didn't tell my mother in a letter. I thought it would be more of a thrill for her to see me on the stage. When she came up for the first night, I didn't meet her before the show. She told me afterwards that, when I walked on and lifted my hat, she said to herself, 'Ash-blonde! Hair like a man! *That*'s not Marjorie!', then, 'It *is* Marjorie, and it's the finest thing she's ever done!'

The comedian of the show was Tommy Lorne. Before Overtures and Beginners he used to burst into the chorus room and shout, 'Come, you's yins! The bugle's went!' I'd to sing 'All by Yourself in the Moonlight' on a fence while he did comedy tricks. With Myrette I sang 'I Can't Give You Anything But Love'. And, while the boat was sinking, I sang 'Ramona' on my own before being saved. To make it look as though I was on the high seas the men at the back had to rock the boat as I clung to a mast with a flag at the top. Everytime I was getting away with 'Ramona – la-*la*-la-la-la-la-la-*la*', the boat rocked and my voice wavered. Very often I was shoved about so much, I couldn't sing at all. The idea was to make a 'picture', with the lights fading till I was out of sight. I used to complain to the boys, 'It's a good job I don't suffer from indigestion! For goodness sake let me get some singing done tonight and don't shake me to bits!' Cruickshank finally came round one night and said, 'I'm not making a complaint about *you*, my dear, but you're not getting half a chance to sing that number. We'll have a rehearsal tomorrow and see if we can improve it.'

We did improve it. From then on, the boys didn't rock my voice at the same time as they rocked the boat.

Early that January, there was snow on the ground, and Victoria Carmen took a violent chill.

I played Principal Boy in her place. At last! MARJORIE GRAHAM was all alone in electric lights outside the King's Theatre, Edinburgh!

Chapter Five

One Sunday in January, two of the chorus girls I was friendly with said they'd never been to the Castle. I said I'd take them there, and afterwards we could come down to tea at the North British Hotel.

It was a cold day, windy and unpleasant. I was explaining about the old guns when a stranger walked past us and then back past us again. He didn't come and speak, or even stay near, but stood some distance away, taking a great interest in our behaviour. One of the girls made a joke about it. 'He's tailing us!', she said. I laughed. 'Just what *I* was thinking! Maybe he's a policeman. Have we done anything wrong?'

We walked down to the North British. I knew the head waiter. He brought us tea and cakes. We were enjoying these and laughing happily when suddenly my eye saw, sitting opposite, the man who had been up at the Castle. 'He *is* following us!' I thought. 'It must be another case of mistaken identity.'

He kept looking over. Then he started smiling. Soon the head waiter came over and said, 'The gentleman opposite asks may he join you.'

We made polite conversation. At the end of tea he offered to drive us home to our various digs.

He drove the other two to theirs first. When we got to mine he said 'May I come in?' It was early in the evening, about six, so I said, 'Certainly!' In he came. I offered him a glass of sherry. He invited me to dine with him at the Royal British. I accepted. He drove me home. When could he see me again?

Every night for a week he came to the stage door and took me out to supper. His name was John Rodger and he was manager of the Canada Life Assurance Company in Castle Street. His clothes were well tailored and he was slim and fair, with broad shoulders. He had a small, very neat moustache and a delightful mouth, beautifully shaped, determined and big. When he spoke, he seemed to use it. It attracted you. Your eyes kept looking at it. His dark brown eyes were not set wide enough apart. That was the only feature I didn't like about him. I didn't mind that he had a stiff leg from being wounded in the war. He was amusing and had an altogether magnetic personality. I fell desperately in love with him.

I became Mrs Rodger on the 11th May, 1930, at Marylebone Register Office. We had lived together at the Grosvenor Hotel, Edinburgh, till the end of the run of *Robinson Crusoe*, when I came back to Blandford Street. I carried beige roses, rather unusual, and wore an olive green dress, a pale green hat and pale green gloves with beige turn-backs. Neil Fielding sent me a present of five pounds.

Our honeymoon at Eastbourne was the most lovely fortnight I've ever spent. I was very much in love with someone who hadn't got a fortune but could keep me comfortably. The hotel was on the front. We were in the bridal suite overlooking the promenade and the sea. Sexually, we got on well. I thought we were two in one. In fact, he almost wanted more than I did at the beginning. Luckily I was healthy and strong and couldn't care less if it happened every half hour. The first evening we had two bottles of champagne. We popped one in the middle of the night and the other before morning.

On the pier he bought me big, stupid dolls. We were like children. We played all those silly games. For instance, I won at shooting though I'd never held a gun. We usually went back for tea and danced. John, despite his limp, could do all the steps that mattered. After dinner, we drank in other hotels and danced again.

Before we went to live on the smarter South Side of Edinburgh, we had a tenement flat in Haymarket Street. We were on the third floor and there was no lift. Naughty messenger boys used to write rude words on the staircase walls – 'bloody', 'shit' and a few other words I knew. Coming up one night with my husband, I said, 'Oh, what does that mean – "f—"?' He said, '*Marjorie*!! You surely know what that means! You've been on the stage! Saying it out like that was disgusting!' I said, 'I don't know what it means at all.' People used to think that because you were on the stage you not only slept with anyone you fancied but also knew what 'f—' meant.

John played golf every Sunday at Dalmahoy, so I tried to learn. I never made a go of it. Instead I walked round the eighteen holes with him and his men friends, joining them in a Sandy Mac from their flasks at every third. Finally I said to John, 'You know, I'd much rather ride. Could I go to riding school? I've a friend who is very keen to learn.' He agreed.

Ruth Kirke and I were like Mutt and Jeff. I was quite a big person and she couldn't have been skinnier. We found a charming instructor at Gilmerton, and three times a week we went over by bus or in her husband's car. Poor little Ruth was so thin she had to have a pony. She hadn't the strength to grip a pony even, and, when she went for a long ride, her bottom got sore. Once, we went over the Braids and she was red raw. Poor soul! She stuck it to the end, but it was too much for her.

I rode well. Like acting, it must have been in the blood. (Daddy was in the Yeomanry.) I was given a jolly big horse – Lorna Doone. Unfortunately she ate a poisonous mushroom and died. Once she threw me bang into a great patch of baggy nettles. I'd a white silk blouse on with short sleeves. The instructor rubbed me with dock leaves. He was keen on me, but I gave him no encouragement.

Ruth and I would finish up at the Haws Inn (known, needless to say, as The Whores Inn) and tag the horses before riding back to the stables. One morning I was given a mare called Daisy, a hefty bit, hard to get on to even when sober. I'd had a couple too many. I couldn't mount. A policeman on point duty helped me make the saddle. I reached the stables at a gallop, hanging round Daisy's neck.

Ruth wasn't very good at any sport, but we played tennis together in the park and went swimming at Portobello where there were ever-cleansing baths with salt water running in and out from the sea.

Though the South Side flat was a good-sized

one, and wasn't modern in any way, I had no maid, I had only a woman three times a week for filling the coal buckets and washing the bathroom and kitchen floors. Every morning in winter I set five coal fires. Then I had to sweep the carpets with cold tea and a brush and shovel. The wireless had a wet battery and a dry battery and you could carry it anywhere – that is, if you had a truck. Thank heavens John rarely came home to lunch! It was enough to have people to dinner three or four times a week.

Dinner was at seven-thirty so, to be ready, I had to be back by five. We had three courses every night – soup, fish and meat. No sweet – just cheese and biscuits or angels-on-horseback. Friends used to say, 'Marjorie, how on earth do you produce a meal like this without any help?!' To be fair, John helped. He would check the table when I set it. I'd say, 'Check, dear!' and there was always a fork missing. Sometimes he'd set the table himself. He always insisted on silver candelabra. He was very good at that sort of thing. I never learned enough about wine. I thought a

Hock was the ankle of an animal. This disappointed him. He said, 'Darling, one should *know* these things!' He kept a good cellar of wine, whisky, gin and 'the condiments' as I call them – orange, lemon, angostura and the like. He could buy cases cheaply through friends. As the marriage continued, I drank more and more.

We never played cards, though whist was all the rage. After dinner, on the evenings we weren't going to the King's or the Lyceum, I sang or played on the piano. 'I'll See You Again' was John's favourite number. He thought I sang marvellously. I thought he told stories marvellously. What is more, to begin with, I believed them to be true. One of his set pieces was about his time in the Seaforths. While under fire in France and already badly wounded in the leg, he was trying to get back to his own lines and got entangled in some barbed wire. He woke up in hospital before being put to bed, and found he was stark naked. 'Where's ma kilt?' he shouted, and they said, 'You left it on the barbed wire!'

Sometimes we danced to the gramophone. With the furniture pushed back, the room could take two or three couples. Sometimes we went dancing at the Caledonian or the North British.

One Christmas at the Caledonian I wore long diamond earrings and a diamond brooch with a black velvet gown which was backless and had a little train that kicked out as one walked or danced. John looked fine in tails. Our host asked us to take the floor and dance the carioca. We received an ovation. I was used to applause, but John lapped it up. He said I was wonderful and beautiful and that all other women were ordinary.

When Nita Croft was starring in *The White Horse Inn* at the King's with Archie Glenn, the comedian, they both came to supper after the show. We all got very high, including Nita who was not used to drinking. She was sitting on a couch with Archie. I was in one armchair. John was in the other. We'd been telling naughty stories. Suddenly, Nita started undoing Archie's buttons and undressing him. Then she slipped her own dress off to the waist (it couldn't go any further as it was tight-fitting lamé) and said, 'Come on, boys!' and started prancing about. In those days that was only done in brothels! John and I were *appalled*!

Mother was lonely, and the sewing in Blandford Street was getting too much for her. She gave up her London flat and arranged to live with us for six months of the year and, for the other six, to look after an invalid friend in Moffat. She was company for me. John was out so much, working supposedly. Often he didn't get back till after midnight. He said he was visiting clients, seeing old farmers in the country about their policies. From a sexual point of view I wasn't getting enough of him. That side of him had fizzled out. I never stopped to ask why. When you are in love with someone, you accept. I just said, 'Bless his heart! He doesn't want to, but he can't help it.' It never entered my head, till later, that he might have other women or a boyfriend even. Many nights I wanted him to come home and have sex with me. Many, many nights. But he'd come home and say, 'Hello, darling! Still awake? Good! Oh, I'm so tired! A farmer gave me a right old binge up! If he hadn't driven me to the station in his car, I'd have missed the last train.' Very often he'd fall asleep while we were talking. I'd lie awake. I'd think, 'He doesn't want me tonight. Maybe that's the way men are.' I didn't know any different. Maybe men didn't feel like I did. Maybe they only wanted sex about once a week. I shrugged the matter off. I loved him just the same. I didn't yet realize that it was my mother who was the only love of my whole life, the only real, the only beautiful love.

I felt neglected. I had to try to tire myself out, keep myself busy flower-arranging, watering my potted plants, riding, swimming, playing tennis. We had no children. I wanted children. Stewart Campbell, a friend of John's who was in the silk business, gave me a present of yards and yards of celanese which my mother made up into sets of pyjamas. Delightful they were, with one colour on top of the other. They intrigued John because most women wore nighties. But they didn't intrigue him enough to prevent me having to sit patiently listening to late-night dance music on the wireless till he got home too tired to be too tired to be too tired.

I missed a period once. Every afternoon I used

to put my feet up, and hope for the best. When the next month came, though, all was well. I thought I'd better go and see a doctor. He just laughed. 'I imagine you caught a chill on one of your rides.' I was very disappointed. Looking back, I don't know that John was.

He was beginning to show signs of impatience with me. He was opening his letters and reading the paper during breakfast. Once, when all my stockings were laddered and I asked him for some money to buy more, he said, 'Good God! You've got a dress allowance. Surely you can buy yourself stockings out of that?!' I said, 'No! I'm afraid I've spent my allowance for this month.' He flung half a crown onto the bed.

That made Mother boil. She saved him money always by making clothes with material she bought herself so that I could look nice entertaining his friends.

But I adored him. Anything he did I could forgive. Once, when he accepted an invitation to dinner as a single man to be paired with another woman, I picked up his silk topper while he was changing and did a high kick through it. It was the finest high kick I ever accomplished. Though I didn't apologize for it aloud, I did so in my heart after he had gone and as I wept and wept on Mumsie's shoulder.

CHAPTER SIX

John often used to go down to London to Canada Life's head office. One day a man came in to the Castle Street Branch and asked to see a policy John had arranged for him. His secretary could find no policy. She rang John at Head Office. 'Oh my goodness!' he said. 'I'm so sorry. I must have mislaid it. I'll see to it personally when I get back.'

The man followed it up. There was no policy. The firm's suspicions were aroused. They began to ferret out that John wasn't running the Castle Street branch properly. He had altered the weekly cheques he received from Head Office to pay his staff, lodged them with his own bank and kept the balance. He had also failed to account for monies received in connection with many of the policies he sold.

Canada Life tried to persuade him to tell just how much he had taken so that he might have a chance to replace it. It was the bank that insisted on prosecution. Canada Life wanted to preserve its good name.

The first thing *I* knew of it all was when John came home one lunchtime. I wasn't expecting him. He said, 'I'm going to give you rather a big shock, I'm afraid.' 'I suppose you've won a fortune on the pools!' I laughed. 'No, dear,' he said, 'I'm perfectly serious.' He walked in to the bedroom, sat down on the bed and – I'll never forget it – announced, 'I've embezzled thirteen thousand pounds.' I said, 'What?! Don't make me laugh! You couldn't get away with *that*!' He said, 'I haven't got away with it. But I did till now.' I said, 'You really mean it?' I still couldn't credit him, I thought he was creating a charade to see my reaction.

When the shock penetrated, I became hysterical. I cried and shouted as if I was going off my head. Thank heavens my mother was there. She helped John to put me to bed. They gave me aspirins, and I slept. When I woke up, I was absolutely numb and able to take the whole thing in my stride.

John told me he was going to London. Would I help him? I did so, naturally. If you love a person you must do something. You can't say, 'No! Go to hell!' I packed all his best clothes so he could sell them if he needed money.

The police came to the flat. They told me I was not bound to tell them anything as I was his wife, but they would appreciate my help. I explained that he had gone to London, giving no address, and that he had cleared his bank account and left me and my mother high and dry with six months of our yearly tenancy still to run.

For a few months he wrote to me from a post office in London. He was a barman in some Soho night-club. He sent no money, only his laundry to wash. Fancy that! Mother tried to stop me, but I had it done and sent it back to him. For the remainder of the tenancy, with the landlord's permission, we ran the flat for four students and cooked them meals.

I wasn't asked to give evidence when John was brought back to Edinburgh. He was sentenced to five years. The trial was in the newspapers. One morning I woke up and I couldn't speak above a whisper. The doctor recommended lots of rest and a holiday in the south of France. That was impossible. Mother and I returned to London on the night bus, the cheapest means there was. We had twenty pounds. We took a flat in Cornwall Street, Pimlico, with one living room, one bedroom and use of lavatory. I registered at the Labour Exchange, and Mother started dressmaking again.

I never saw John from that day till the day he died. I didn't even know he had died till I went to my solicitors for a divorce in order to marry my second husband. I never went to see him in prison. My whole life, my whole being, everything in me was part of him and I felt it my duty to go, but Mother said to do so would be my ruin. He wrote to me occasionally from prison without any sign of love or devotion. He never said, 'Don't let me down. I promise when I get out to make it up to you.' The only letter I wrote to him asked for a divorce, and he replied beseeching me to wait for at least another year when, due to good library work, he might be on parole.

He had always pretended his mother was dead. He wore arm-bands when the anniversary of her death came round. I thought it such a lovely gesture. We used to have a quiet dinner specially. Now I discovered she was alive, living in a bungalow in Tiverton, near Manchester. I wrote to her. She invited me to stay. She waited on me hand and foot. She was sorry that her one and only adorable John had done this terrible thing to me. It hurt her deeply to learn he had pretended she was dead. She told me her bungalow and furniture were given by a Jewish family for whom she had worked as a lady's maid. She gave her own furniture to John, thinking he was living in a bachelor's apartment. Until I wrote to her she didn't know that he was married. I began to wonder – had every moment of our eight years together been founded on lies? About the divorce proceedings she said, 'It would be kind if you *did* listen to what John asks you, and not be in a hurry since he wants probation. I'll keep in touch with you and let you know how things go.' So every now and then she wrote to me and I wrote to her, until one of my letters was returned 'Deceased', and I lost trace of John forever.

All I had wanted in life was to be with John and to do what he wanted to do. I worshipped him, every bit of him. I never questioned him. Good Lord! You don't keep a man on a string! Before meeting him I had ideas of being a star in the theatre. I wanted to be famous. I wanted the public to like me. Then none of these things seemed to matter. I broke my contract. What he said, I did. He had me under his power. He could have done anything he wanted with me. If he'd asked me to go East or West or to do this or to do that, I'd have been only too pleased. He was working for me at the office, so I tried to work for him at home.

Mother couldn't understand me loving John still. She said that my faith in God must be stronger, that I must be a better Christian than she; she'd never felt for anyone that awful hatred she now felt for him. This is what she told me: 'Marjorie, if John should walk into this flat, be it day or night, don't be surprised if I attempt to put a knife in his back, because that's just what I will do!'

I had often longed for a child by John. Now Mother said, 'God was good to you. We'd have been three to keep instead of two.' In this I think her attitude was right.

Chapter Seven

My voice came back gradually. It was no longer mezzo-soprano. It was baritone. I couldn't go back on the stage. I had lost my nerve. People said I'd be marvellous on the radio, but I hadn't the strength to try. I felt finished. I felt that everything I had done in life and everything I believed in had crashed. I didn't want to go on. I drank beer to blot it all away. But when I woke all my problems returned. I recommend drink if it does you good or if you like it. I don't recommend it as an escape. Mother saved me from becoming an addict like my father. She said, 'That's the coward's way out! You and I can get over this if you pull yourself together and realize it's not the end of the world. You're a young woman with a big life ahead of you.'

The first job the Exchange gave me was steam-hand at the ABC. I didn't know what 'steam-hand' was. I used to think it was something to do with pressing pants. I sailed along to the corner of Wilton Road, and into the Staff Entrance round the back in the Vauxhall Bridge Road where Flanagan's Betting Shop is now. I announced I was their new steam-hand. I wasn't questioned. I was told there were uniforms up-stairs, and found a white overall and a little white cap. Then I was told to report to the manageress in the basement. I went down to the basement thinking, 'I've never done this sort of thing before. I've never met this kind of people. I've never been in the back of a café in my life. But – hurray! – I've got a job.'

I saw urns everywhere. Someone was banging down the handles of a machine that went 'Psss, Psss!' That it was *my* machine didn't occur to me even then. Up came the manageress, a charming person. 'Oh, you're the new steam-hand. I'll give you over to this girl here. She'll put you right. You'll soon get into it. It's very simple. At first, perhaps, you'll be slow, but you'll soon discover how quick you can be.'

I was pushed behind two urns – one for coffee and one for milk. There was a big pipe in the middle and I had to bang it to make boiling water come down. At the foot was a grid where the water ran away. There were clean cups in rows which I had to fill with coffee or tea when the waitresses came up and put a chit on them. The tea was not in an urn except during busy times. I made it in a fresh pot. I got so quick I could do six or twelve cups in one sweep of the hand. Hot stuff! The first day, of course, I thought I'd never be able to do it. But within a week I was head girl! The manageress saw someone, I suppose, with a bit of intelligence. A terrible class of person was there – decent souls, but no brains whatever.

There were two shifts: six till three and, the next day, three till ten. You got one day off. I was paid a pittance, no more than two pounds a week. Living only ten minutes away helped. Also, you got your food and you could have got drunk on tea and coffee if you wanted to.

Men I met at Auntie Day's helped me pick up the threads of life again. I was introduced to Mr Indermaur, a property owner, who finally got Mother and me out of Cornwall Street. 'Mr Indermaur,' I said, 'we've got bugs!' He went to our landlord and made him fumigate while we stayed for a day at my aunt's. That made things all right for the winter. But when summer came we were as bad as before. In the mornings there'd be blood all over the sheets where I'd scratched myself and squeezed the bugs. If you got up quick in the night and put the light on, you'd see them all over the bed, running. You killed as many as you could, and got some peace for a while. I told Indermaur again. He said, 'The house needs burning down.'

The next time I saw Indy, as we soon called him, he said, 'I've got a basement for you in St George's Drive. One of my tenants has been taken away to prison.' We were established there within a week. There was an unfinished meal on the table in the kitchen which was to become our living room. I've been in this flat ever since.

Indy was a German-Swiss, or shall we say a Swiss-German. He had come to this country, done very well in the catering business and bought himself three houses. We were in one of them. Every Sunday at twelve o'clock he called for his twenty-five shillings rent – twenty-five shillings for a basement flat with lots of concessions such as delving in the garden and hanging out the washing which I'm not allowed today by the woman who took over.

I think Indy may have had an eye for me. Anyway, when he had collected the rent, he always said, 'Come on! We're off to Mrs Ingram's!' (Mrs Ingram ran the Marquis Pub.) It became a joke between Mother and me that, by the time we came out, Indy had spent the rent money – on us!

Now Mother drank Scotch and I drank beer, preferably draught mild and bitter. One day, Indy said, 'You can't go on drinking that beer, Marjorie! Have a Scotch like your mother!' I said, 'I don't care for Scotch!' He said, 'Have you ever tried it with a little milk?'

Well! I got so *keen*! A good double filled to the

top with milk. I do it yet. Right till Mrs Ingram died I used to walk along to the Marquis with a pint of milk under my arm.

At one of my aunt's tea parties my mother met a very beautiful woman. Her name was Billy Forman. She had posed for photographs in debutantes' feathers and written gossip for the magazines. She had even understudied Diana Manners in *The Miracle*. She gave me a watercolour portrait of Jessie Matthews by Hannay – also a hand-embroidered Spanish shawl in beigy pink with a deep fringe, a memento of theatrical days. It hangs in my sitting-room still and I often wear it as a wrap.

Billy was getting on. She had retired and was 'hostess' at the Metropole, Victoria. She stood impressively in the hall in an enormous black cloak like Dracula and met people as they arrived. For ten per cent of takings, she got Mother the job of lavatory attendant in the same cinema.

Until then there had been an ordinary cleaner who went into the lavs and wiped the seats, but Billy said to Mother, 'It may sound menial, Mrs

Hunter, but if you let me explain everything to you I think you'll find it very lucrative. You'll get a small salary of twenty-five shillings a week, and can run the place exactly as you like. Don't charge, but put out a saucer and people will put in their money as they feel inclined. You'll be surprised how the pennies will add up after three shows a day. It's certainly not hard work; you can read and do your sewing, and I'll always see you right about a cup of tea.'

Mother made a success of it. She displayed Janet Moore cosmetics. She gave everyone personal attention. During the intervals, the 'breaks', she went in ahead of her patrons carrying a white towel and saw that the lavatory was clean – or affected to do so. To begin with, she wore a white overall. She looked like a nurse. Later, when a new manager arrived, he suggested that, as she ran the place so beautifully, she wear a black frock and keep her ten per cent.

Meanwhile, being a steam-hand was boring me stiff. I got work at the Astoria, a great big dance hall in Charing Cross Road. It was middle class, the Astoria – not quite 'West End'.

I was chef's commy in the kitchen. I could hear the dance band outside. The doors opened straight on to it. It was bang, bang, bang, bang – 'When You're Smiling' and so on. When the waitresses came in with their orders, I couldn't hear for the noise and they had to scream. At first I thought, 'I can't stick this!' But, do you know, after less than a fortnight I used to hear every word those waitresses said, and I couldn't hear what the band was playing! Yet it was *booming*! The leader used to come in for his cup of tea. He asked once, 'Did you like that new number?' I said, 'What new number?'

The manager of the Astoria was a Jew. The chef and he were always fighting about how the meat should be cooked. In the end I got them to be friends. 'What's the good of fighting?' I said. 'Why not you, Chef, cook it your way one night, and let the manager give the orders the next? Then see what the customers liked best.' They thought that was a good idea.

There were hectic parties after work. One was given by a waitress nicknamed Bloody Mary – a darling soul, Welsh, but who couldn't say one sentence without using a 'bloody'. 'Bloody tea for two and hurry up!' Well, at this bottle party of hers, I noticed all the crockery and cutlery belonged to the Astoria. She stole some every day.

I could always get a good crowd to my place in St George's Drive because I had a piano. Once, we were the saxophonist, the drums, the pianist from the Astoria, waitresses, me, Mother, two policemen in uniform, pub friends . . . The piano top was wet with beer and gin. I opened it and a drunk poured his glass inside. By dawn we were laid out on the floors, on the beds, along the corridor and in the bath.

We thought Pat on the Cold Bar was a bit homosexual, but during my stay he announced he was going to marry a girl who appeared normal in every way. He invited Mother and me to the reception. I've never been to such a terrible reception in my life. The people! I've never met such ruffians! Poor Mother! She didn't know where to turn. They put their cups on the plates and stuck their spoons in the cups or chucked them on the white tablecloths.

Pat always used to say, 'Marjorie, what are you

doing of?' I stood it for quite some time, then took him aside. 'Pat, darling,' I told him, 'I wish you wouldn't keep saying "doing of". There's no "doing of" anything. You just say "doing".' He said, 'Thank you, Marjorie, very much. I know my grammar's bad. Any time I say anything else wrong I'd be most grateful if you'd help me.' I could have wept. He was so nice about it I wished I hadn't spoken.

But he still went on saying 'doing of', and I had to check, check, check him. I may have cured him eventually, but I nearly caught the disease myself in the process. It's so easy to copy others. I got into the habit like the rest of plonking a cup on the table of the Astoria kitchen. At a tea party given by my mother I was telling a tale and, while I did so, picked up my cup, took a sip from it and plonked it on the table. Mother looked at me and said, 'What's wrong with the saucer?' I didn't know I'd done it.

CHAPTER EIGHT

War was declared on Sunday, the 3rd of September, 1939, and the Astoria was taken over as an air-raid shelter. After lunching on duck and green peas, Mother and I took a bus to Charing Cross Road. I got my stuff from my locker and found out what to do about my money. The staff made farewells at the local pub. Some took addresses. At closing time we drifted apart.

Enid Trevor, Claude Hulbert's wife, came to the rescue. She found me a job as housekeeper to Miss Cicely Courtneidge, Claude's sister-in-law, in South Audley Street.

'She's a very peculiar and difficult woman,' Enid warned me before the interview. 'She may take a violent dislike to you as she did to me when I wanted to marry Claude. Don't be disappointed if she says, "You'll be hearing from me," which will mean you won't. But here are a few tips: Let her take the stage. Don't be your usual chattery self. Flare out only when she asks you questions to show you're not illiterate and dumb.'

The house had a very impressive front. I rang the bell. A manservant answered. I was shown into an attractive study, the study I was going to have to clean and polish afterwards, which was a difficult and different matter.

Miss Courtneidge kept me waiting for a while, then made her entrance, full of her usual vivacity. She talked and talked and talked, and I let her have the stage as Enid advised. Would I take some tea? 'Oh,' I thought, 'it doesn't look as though she's taken a *violent* dislike!'

We got on beautifully. Not only was she charming, she was most generous. If she was having a cocktail party, she'd give her staff a drink beforehand, mixed by herself. If you did overtime, she'd instruct her secretary to give you extra money without your asking. Once she bought a bear-skin rug. She laid it down in the drawing-room and called for my opinion. I said, 'What a lovely rug, Miss Courtneidge!' She said, 'I think it's hideous in here. Take it away if it's any good to you!' Also, when the washable glass-topped trays for drink came in, she gave me two beautiful mahogany ones. They were only slightly soiled by mats.

She was very keen on flowers. There was a grand piano in the drawing-room. On one end was nothing but vases of flowers – roses, carnations, expensive flowers ordered daily, not to mention her bouquets. She was the first person I knew to have plastic flowers. They were done by a person from outside who put them in special niches up the stairway and changed them every month. Exotic pastries she loved, too. She'd pop me in a taxi to go and buy them for her in a Belgian shop. And *parsley*! It was always on the shopping list among the greens. 'Get a *big* bunch!' she'd say. There had to be pieces of parsley on the butter, pieces of parsley round the dishes. It was a sort of madness.

Apart from dusting, hoovering, laying the table, polishing the silver and washing up, I was Miss Courtneidge's lady's maid. I warmed her room, met her when she returned from the theatre, carried her things upstairs, got out her slippers. I made sure the house was blacked out. For some reason a policeman used to come each evening to see if this was done properly, then stayed to supper. I served Miss Courtneidge her morning tea at 8.30 and left at eleven. The manservant left with me. He lived in Pimlico, too, so I didn't need to be afraid of the darkness.

One evening Miss Courtneidge and her husband Jack invited Mrs Bobby Howes, Enid, Claude and Alan Melville to dinner. That morning she came to me and said, 'Would you oblige me tonight by waiting at table?' I said, 'Oh, Miss Courtneidge, I've never waited at table in my life! I can bring the stuff in from the kitchen and put it on the sideboard, but to actually *wait* . . .!' 'Nonsense!' she said. 'You know to go from the left and to the right?' 'Well,' I said, 'I've *seen* it done.' 'I'll give you a rehearsal,' she said. 'Of course you'll do it! You'll do anything for me, won't you?!' That was the lovely way she had. I said, 'I'll probably make a mess of it.' She said, 'Who cares, anyway? What does it matter? I'll give you a nice little apron and make you attractive, and you'll be fine!' She talked me into it.

I was terrified. It was like a first night. The soup and the fish went well. But, sure enough, when the middle course came and I went round with the vegetables, I reached Alan Melville and knocked the cauliflower spoon onto the floor. I started to bend down. He said, 'Not at all, my dear! I'll get it.' 'Alan always to the rescue!' said Miss Courtneidge. They were sweet. Kind and considerate as usual, Miss Courtneidge came out to the kitchen afterwards and gave me a drink.

During the War it was very hard to get washing-up powder. Such as there was, and Miss Courtneidge got plenty, contained too much soda. My fingers started to irritate. I had to show them to her and tell her I'd better not come in to work. She made me an appointment there and then with her specialist in Harley Street.

I was sitting in the waiting-room when who should walk in but my sweetheart, of old, Neil Fielding, the father of my baby. What a coincidence! He'd come to have a check-up on his heart. For ten minutes we talked. He took me by the hand. But there was no feeling of wanting him back. Too much had happened since I loved him. I think he was affected more than I was.

The job with Cicely Courtneidge lasted over a year and ended with her giving up the house. For the next two years I worked night shifts, serving sandwiches in the Civil Defence Corps canteen, Charing Cross Road. As time went on, the men were called out to more and more incidents. A bomb dropped on top of the Palladium and didn't explode. Someone crawled out onto the roof and took the bomb away to be defused. In those days it was considered a great feat. The same man, when the Guildhall, Pimlico, half fell over and the rest wouldn't collapse, went up in a crane, after the people round about were evacuated, and demolished the building with explosives. After the war, he got the George Medal.

Every house in St George's Drive had shelters

under the road with beds, mattresses and electric light. No one would use them because they were so damp. Some used an enormous shelter behind Victoria Station where there is a bus depot now. A bomb dropped on it and four hundred people were buried alive. Every night when she got back from the Metropole, Mother invited the people in the house down to the basement, or the Dug-Out as she christened it. When there was an alert, she hid behind the piano. I warned her that if anything went off it would fall on top of her and she'd be killed. I used to walk from the Dug-Out to Charing Cross Road in a crash helmet. One night I counted seven fires on the way and, when I got to my destination, found it waterlogged and firemen pumping water out of the basement area where a bomb had landed and started another fire.

Blasts are strange things. A bomb once dropped solidly right opposite the Dug-Out on the corner house of Warwick Square. The blast went over the gardens of the Square and only shattered our windows. Another time, Mother and I were in the Marquis at the other end of the Square and a bomb dropped on the corner house opposite that.

On this occasion the blast came towards us –
wallop! One moment we were sitting drinking,
the next we were flat on the floor. To be blown
out of a cannon must feel the same. But what was
so extraordinary was this. The glasses and bottles
on the tables hadn't budged, yet the impact had
been so great that all the windows of the pub
were smashed. A terrible incident was said to
have taken place three streets away from St
George's Drive. The residents of about five houses
were found sat dead, with food on the table as if
they were still eating their supper. Again, it was
the impact from a bomb which didn't hit the
houses concerned but a building nearby.

I went to the post office in the Vauxhall Bridge
Road in the blackout one Christmas with a
bundle of cards and presents. The post office was
shut. I was coming back along Churton Street
and heard a doodle-bug flying low. It went right
over me, stopped in front, and made a hole in the
middle of Belgrave Road. The impact threw me
on my face. I was furious. The knees were put out
of both my silk stockings and I had to crawl fish-
ing around for my cards and parcels.

After the Civil Defence Corps, I joined the American Red Cross.

My first job with the Americans was at Batt's Club, Dover Street, a club for the women who drove motor-lorry canteens to the American camps. I was chamber maid in charge of a floor of bedrooms. Sometimes, to make a bit extra, I relieved the operator on the switchboard. The women tipped well. Money was no object to the Americans at all.

That lasted six months. Then I was transferred to Jules Club for GIs in Jermyn Street. I was given another floor of bedrooms there. Every night when you left the canteen you were given a fresh bag of doughnuts. I'd never seen ringed ones till the Americans brought them over.

Young men would arrive on my floor. I'd look at my list and say, 'This is your room, sir.' They'd put a bottle of whisky or gin on the table and say, 'Haven't you got any glasses?'! They were just as generous with cigarettes. I started smoking Camels heavily.

GIs took me drinking in the evening – to Raynor's Bar where they sold rum and cloves, an

American favourite, and to the Chequers at the back of Jules in an old cobbled yard where I'd to walk gingerly in my high heels. They looked smart in their forage caps and beige. I had an affair with one or two – rooms in Soho after dinner downstairs. But that was war-time, nothing stuck. For me, it didn't matter. Drink was more important than sex. It gave me the pep to go on. I'm sure it was with the Red Cross I began to *need* whisky. The odd GI would say, 'I've had you out all evening, now what about it?' But when you said, 'I'm sorry, that wasn't in the contract. I just came out to drink', they never made any scenes. Americans are fine, very considerate to women. I got a very good impression of them all. When they made a pass and realized you weren't out to sell your body, they didn't ditch you before seeing you home. An Englishman would have said 'Bye, sister.'

Later I joined Jules' Officers' Annexe. I was responsible for fewer rooms, and didn't have to scrub and polish floors.

The boys had already started celebrating when I arrived at 8.30 on D-Day. I should think they'd already downed a couple of bottles apiece. Nobody worked that day at all. The beds weren't made. Cigarettes, Canadian Rye, maids, managers, officers . . . We reached the stage where we were aiming bottles long range through the windows into a compound over the road. Then we had drinks at the Chequers. I got so lit I don't remember getting to lunch. By evening we were back at the Chequers, laughing, doing high kicks on the tables, singing the Star Spangled Banner, collapsing in corners . . . Mother thought there had been an accident when four officers carried me down the basement steps and dumped me down on the couch, out for the count. I woke next morning with a frothy tongue, a mouth like the bottom of a parrot's cage, and feeling I had died quietly.

The club continued for about six months. Then staff were given a farewell dinner and floorshow: drinking galore, balloons, crackers, petals from the roof, two bands. No Vera Lynn!

CHAPTER NINE

Mother had a spinster friend, a dispenser in an East End hospital, who offered me two hours' housework a week. They met at the Marquis through the Reverend Crow, always full of boy-pranks and defrocked twice for soliciting in Victoria Station. She recommended me to the head porter at Dolphin Square. This led to other things. In the end I must have been working for a dozen people.

There was a retired naval captain. Should he come in when I was cleaning he'd say, 'Why not sit down and have a drink?' There was a German lady, a teetotaller. She had a clever, attractive son who offered me whiskies. Another lady, who writes to me from Eastbourne to this day, said, 'My husband works for Curtis's Gin. Have you heard of them?' I answered the truth which was No. 'Are they a big firm?' I asked. 'The only gins I know are Gordon's and Booth's.' She said, 'Curtis's aren't even as well known as Beefeater's, and I just hope you can drink it because it's the most terrible stuff. We only drink it ourselves because we get it for nothing.' She suggested I add plenty of orange or lemon so as not to taste it. Gin isn't my favourite tipple, even with peppermint. It makes me morbid. I become entirely different to my usual personality which is cheerful and optimistic. I was once the life and soul of a party and made everybody roar because gin had made me so terribly miserable. I reclined on a big couch with lots of cushions and started to tell the story of my life and how everyone hated me and it wasn't fair. Then I picked up a cushion and buried my head in it and wept and everybody began to laugh. 'You all laugh,' I said, pushing the cushion away, 'but you don't know what it is to be sad!' Apparently it was the funniest thing that any of the guests had ever seen.

Next door to the Curtis's Gin people lived a grunty old girl with arthritis, a bad heart and cancer of the breast. She was brought up in France. I had to shop for her, make the bed and wash the dishes. At the beginning she was very aloof, very much on guard, as if to suggest, 'I don't know if I like you or if I don't.' I thought, 'After all, if she treats me decently, she's a couple of hours' work.' In the end we became very fond of one another. She used to sit me down, when I should have been working, and talk about the theatre. She had been in amateur theatricals and had read the theatrical biographies, knew who was the daughter of So and So, and who was married to whom. She was very much the old lady of the past. She didn't like the people who called at the door to be familiar and address her as 'duckie' or 'darling'. She said, 'I'm not used to servants calling me that! Are there no manners nowadays?!' She dropped ash every-where. Crumbs and dust were nothing to the ash. And she was always very tight with money. I had to account in writing for the shopping. She told me not to buy a tinned soup at one shop because it was twopence off at another, so I had to go trailing an extra distance. When she lost the attachment to an earring, she wore one earring for a year rather than go to the expense of having the other mended.

I also worked as a help for Mr and Mrs Williams of Ashley Gardens. Mrs Williams' stage name was Barbara Leigh. She was singing in *King's Rhapsody* at the Palace, and understudying the main part. When rehearsing she used to say to me, 'Stop the dusting and play the piano for me!' Her husband, David Williams, was in *South Pacific* at Drury Lane.

In the end, though, I dropped everyone in favour of an all-day job with Thorley Walters, found (again) through Enid Trevor. Like most theatrical people he was terribly untidy. I was as good as a valet to him. He'd have a shower, then leave everything on the floor all wet for me to pick up. He was immaculate and very handsome. He invited Mother and me to Ivor Novello's last show at the Adelphi – *Gay's the Word* – in which Cicely Courtneidge sang 'Vitality'. We sat next to Ivor's box, a great thrill for both of us.

There's a story about the Metropole at this time that Mother loved to tell. A Miss Hyde ran the café. After work, or outside the 'breaks', the two of them used to cross to the Grosvenor Hotel for drinks. Miss Hyde had wealthy friends who met there, and Mother was usually asked to join the party. One night Miss Hyde introduced her to some strangers, and one of them got talking to her personally while Miss Hyde was sat on her other side. 'I understand you work at the Metropole, Mrs Hunter?' 'Yes,' said Mother brightly, 'I've got a very nice job. I . . .' Before she could say another word in butted Miss Hyde with, 'It's in our Powder Room. Have you ever been to the Metropole?' 'No, as a matter of fact I haven't,' said the woman. 'Well,' said Miss Hyde 'the Powder Room is a most marvellous place. It's got all *manner* of things.' Mother couldn't have cared less, but Miss Hyde didn't want to come down in the world socially.

Mother died in 1953. She was seventy-nine and pronounced as having cancer.

One evening, when she came back from duty, she didn't want her supper. She felt sick and had a pain in her stomach. She took bicarbonate of soda in boiling water, thinking it was indigestion.

Next morning the pain was still there. I called the doctor. The doctor recommended expert advice. I took her by bus to Westminster Hospital for examination.

The surgeon asked to see me privately. He wanted permission to operate. 'Your mother is suffering from cancer of the abdomen and rectum. The operation will be a big one, but her heart and lungs are healthy, I'm sure she'll pull through.'

She was kept in. She was so sensible. She didn't complain. I went home to get her everything she wanted – her nightie, dressing-gown, slippers, face things and denture powder.

I visited her for a fortnight. The operation involved a hole in the side to let the excretions out. The hole had to be regularly cleaned and dressed. The surgeon told me she had only six months to live. 'I guarantee one thing,' he said. 'She won't suffer any pain.'

She went to a convalescent home in Swanley to learn how to use the contraption in her side. It was too far away for me to visit. She wrote me a letter every day. 'Oh, please, when can I come home?' she said. 'I want to come home *so* badly! All the people here are strange and I haven't the strength to talk to them. I just want to come home to you, darling. Please come and take me!'

Those two sincere friends, Claude and Enid Hulbert, brought their Jaguar to the door, drove me down to Mother and brought us both back. I'll never forget that kindness.

On the divan in our big room she was happy as a queen. The GP let her smoke and she picked at a bit of bread and butter and drank Glucozade. When she could get up and look after herself, I took over her job at the Metropole. To set her mind at rest, I told her it was only till she was better. All I had to do for her was her shopping. She never went out, but she cooked me a meal and sewed. She was determined to work till the end of her life.

Towards the end of the six months she got so weak that she had to stay in bed. A nurse came in every day. Her one worry was, 'Am I nice and clean?' The doctor started injecting her with a new drug. 'Till now,' he said, 'the drug we have used for cancer to dull the pain has given the patient horrifying dreams. This gives beautiful and lovely dreams. We call it the Happy Drug. I will gradually increase the dose to make her comfortable. I can tell you the very day she will die. Whenever she wakes, let her drink anything she asks. She won't want to eat.'

The manager of the Metropole let me stay at home to look after her. 'We'll be only too grateful to hold the job for you till you come back,' he said.

Mother must have known she was dying. She never mentioned it, but, before the final week, she wrote a note for me saying she wanted to be cremated.

I stayed beside her. Whenever she woke I was there to hold her hand.

The night before she was to have the last injection, she called out to me, 'A spoonful of water . . . I feel very weak!' I got the water quickly. 'Would you like a little whisky?' I asked, thinking her heart was troubling her. She shook her head. 'Funny, but Mumsie doesn't want that!' I put her hand in mine. My other hand was rested, dangling over the top of the chair beside her bed. I smiled. 'Oh, Mumsie, do you feel *so* weak?' She said, 'No, I'll be all right. I'll be all right.'

Light was coming through the window. It was early morning. She said in a whisper, 'This is a beautiful room, darling. I'll never leave it, even if I die, and I must die soon . . . One door will shut for you and some other one will open . . .' 'No, no! Please, God!' I cried, and I was weeping loudly. 'Not now! No!' I prayed. I prayed most fervently. And, I swear, some hand, there was a hand took mine, my loose one, and grasped it tightly to give me strength.

Mother didn't die that night. She went to sleep and was comfortable and warm. She died next day, on Coronation Eve. Before she died, she woke and said, 'Marjorie!' and then just shut her eyes again for ever.

She is still with me. She governs my life. I believe she walks beside me, as in the words of the old song. She was my greatest love.

CHAPTER TEN

I reigned at the Metropole for twelve years. I thought I'd want to change in a few weeks. I hated the idea of lavatories. I'd done all sorts of funny jobs, but I wasn't happy about this one at all. Soon, though, I was busy making improvements, even on the arrangements made by my mother which had been beneficial in every way.

The manager was a most attractive Scotsman. One night when we were drinking at the Bag O'Nails he said, 'You've got just as much personality as your mother who seemed indispensable. We do miss her terribly, but you're younger and I think you'll make a go of it. I'd like you to stay.'

There was an entrance from the Stalls as well as the Circle. He closed the Stalls entrance because people had to wait over-long in the two queues. Stalls patrons from then on had to use the two unattended lavs, downstairs, so I had the patrons from the most expensive seats. He also put in new roller towels, tip-up liquid soap containers, a huge mirror, pink basins to replace the old-fashioned white, and three new lavs, making four in all. I had a window which opened outwards, which was nice in summer, and a very big cupboard with my own key where at night I kept my brush and comb, hand mirror and clothes brush. Whereas Mother had to sit with her feet on a footstool to keep them out of the draught from the two doors across the stone floor, I had a carpet and now only the one door which was double so that, when the inside one swished open, the other had swished closed and I felt nothing. The cupboard was between the two doors.

I had to be in attendance when the house opened and during 'breaks', but I did not have to stay till the end at night. Before I went home I didn't have to disinfect the bowls and floor. There were cleaners to do that. I just cleaned the mirror with Windolene, scoured the basins with Vim and washed out my little towel with some of the liquid soap. The head ticket-collector brought me fresh towels for the rollers and took away the dirty ones whenever I asked. I wore a black frock – black never goes wrong. The manager asked my measurements and had it made for me. I installed fresh flowers at my own expense – mostly gladioli purchased at first from Moyses Stevens and then cut-price from the barrow opposite.

I was given a basic salary – as much as two pounds in the end. Tips in the saucer added up to a pound on a bad day. With a film like *Lawrence of Arabia*, which ran for four years and was always packed out, I could make an average of two, just in coppers. Nicer people might, of course, leave a shilling. Friends sometimes left more. Dorothy Paget, whom Mother knew well, would come in looking a mess in her old pulled-down hat and trench coat and with a glamorous blonde. She left half a crown.

It was a lovely job. I was my own boss, and I

could sit in the circle and watch the films, then dash back to my cubby-hutch when the 'break' was due.

I never rested in my chair till all four lavs were spotless, not a drip anywhere. I wiped each seat with a towel gripped in the hand. I'd say, 'This way, Madam, I've seen to this one,' and usher her in. Nice people pulled the chain, some never bothered. As soon as they came out, I went in, pulled the chain if necessary and checked for dribbles while they were powdering their noses. On a busy night, every bit of the mirror would be taken with women making-up, washing their hands, fiddling with their hair. I might have six. When they were leaving they'd say, 'How much do I owe you?' I'd say, 'Nothing, Madam. This is free. But there *is* a saucer if you care.' I did my piece. I said it beautifully. Some were flummoxed. They opened their mouths and gaped at me. I felt I ought to explain I was the attendant. I flatter myself that I was more like a theatre attendant which, even then, was always a better type.

During the run of *Lawrence of Arabia*, a most beautiful Indian came in. I couldn't do my job for looking at her. She was like something out of a storybook come to life. She stood in the queue like everybody else. As she passed me she said, 'When I come out I want to talk to you about this film and hear what you think of it.' I was rather taken aback that this gorgeous thing in a sari should suddenly choose to speak to me.

She waited until only a couple of people were left, then she said, 'I'd like to ask you, I'm sure you've heard the opinions of lots and lots of people, what do the majority think of *Lawrence*?' I said, 'It goes without saying what the majority think. Almost four years we've been running with it and there are still packed houses all the time.' 'And what do you yourself think about it?' I said, 'The camel attack – I've watched that again and again. And I *love* the music, I know it off by heart.' She said, 'Thank you. I like to know everyone's opinion because I'm the wife of David Lean, the director.' I hadn't said I knew that Lawrence was short in stature and not very handsome and that O'Toole looked nothing like him. Not that she'd have minded. She wanted the truth.

On big nights special invitations were sent out.

The opening of *Lawrence* was celebrities and nothing else. Princess Margaret and her ladies-in-waiting came, but they never visited me. A special room was curtained off and a lavatory put in. I was disappointed. All I could do was stand in the hall with the usherettes and watch the royal party arrive and walk inside over the red carpet. Everyone gave silver that night. I don't know if they thought it was for charity, but nobody asked questions, certainly the manager didn't, and we had a party at the Bag O' Nails on the proceeds.

There was a very attractive waitress in the cafe called Irish Kathleen. She used to come and see me more often than was perhaps strictly permitted. I became very fond of her. She used to be a hairdresser in the North and, before that, a bus-driver, but she was enticed to London by a Spaniard. He treated her badly for many years. He was a head waiter. I don't think he had ever eaten off a plate. I met him once and took a violent dislike to him. He was trying to be English and to talk like an Etonian: 'What will you have to drink? The sky's the limit, you know!' He wasted all his money on betting. She had to have an abortion because he never told her, till too late, that he was already married to a nice ordinary woman in Madrid and that he had three children. I said, 'Why do you go on with it, Kathleen?' She said, 'Don't ask me! I wish I knew!' 'I don't like him!' I said. 'Most people don't,' she said, 'but unfortunately I do.' He left her. I've lost trace of her – all I have of her is a tartan scarf she gave me. Once she put two pounds in my hand after tea together in Oxford Street, and left me standing. I called, 'Kathleen! Come back! You're not to do that!' But she just waved her hand in the crowd and was gone. The last I heard was she had to be taken to hospital, mentally deranged.

Smithy, an usherette, used to pop up when she had ten minutes. She'd sit on the footstool and I'd sit in my chair and we'd have drinks from my cupboard which was always well stocked with gin and whisky. *She* drank gin. When we heard someone coming, she put her glass down on the floor and put her leg over it. I put mine behind the vase.

Staff used to meet at the Shakespeare opposite.

Smithy and I went there often. There might be as many as six of us off-duty in the Shakespeare at a given time. Another lot might then take over, with me as a link present all the time. That was the beauty of my job. I could be in the Shakespeare when I wanted. Nobody knew when I was in or out. The manager couldn't know, unless he sent somebody up to investigate, which he never troubled to do. If I wanted to get out and not be seen, I could go out the back and come in from the back. I could even come in from the front and he wouldn't know how long I'd been away. I might have been off for two hours. Besides, he only stood in the hall for an hour after the show had started. After that, Chief, the doorman, was put in charge, and he wouldn't have told if I was out all the time. The Shakespeare became a kind of club. We had our own corner table. Even on days off we met there. No one was allowed to pay two rounds on end.

Not everything was pleasant, of course. There were boys of ten or eleven who used to climb the outside staircase and peer into the lavs. Ladies getting off the seat would turn round and see faces. They'd shout, 'Go away, you naughty boys!' or, according to the type, 'Get to hell out of here, you little buggers!' Then I had my regular girls on the beat. It wasn't my job to say, 'Where is your ticket?' If they were nicely dressed they could come right through the front hall and up to me. I've seen them spend an hour washing and titivating themselves. They'd use all my personal equipment, which annoyed me, and never put a halfpenny in the saucer.

One *awful* incident was this. The manager asked me would I sometimes go downstairs to the stalls to the two small lavs, outside which were a mirror, a little basin and a bin for paper towels. He said, 'When you're slack, maybe once in the evening, see the place hasn't got messed up and give it service.'

Down I went one evening. There was paper on the floor. I said to myself, 'Oh, you dirty lot!' and banged my foot on the pedal of the bin. Up went the lid. There was a huge bundle inside, right up to the top and covered with masses of paper towels. I thought, 'Whatever's that? It looks like a parcel!' I lifted it up and out fell a dead baby. I daren't scream because of the film, but I went running to the nearest usherette. 'Please, please come!' I said. 'There's a terrible thing!' I was hysterical.

That baby stuck with me for a very long time. I dreamed about it. I talked about it again and again.

Unfortunately, a new manager at the Metropole made my retirement an unhappy one. Five months before it, just at Christmas time, I asked for compassionate leave of two days as a relative was critically ill. The manager said, 'That is absolutely impossible!' I said, 'I haven't asked many favours. Will you please write up to Head Office?' He replied, 'I only say one thing to you, and that is "Take Christmas off and retire at once!"' I took the time off, and he carried out his threat.

When May, the proper time for my retirement, arrived I went down to the office to collect the money due to me. The manager's secretary, a charming girl, said there was to be a party given in my honour and that the staff had put some money towards a present. What would I like? I said, 'Do you know what would be most useful and what I've least of? Sheets!' So I asked for a pair of sheets and a pair of pillowcases in pink. 'But I only want a party on one condition,' I said, 'and that is that the manager doesn't make the presentation.' She said, 'I understand. I will ask to make the presentation myself. I'm quite sure he'll let me.'

The party was arranged for nine o'clock in the manager's office during the show. All the staff agreed to be there when the show was over, but the presentation, the start of the party, was to be earlier.

I wore plain black, which I always look my best in. I hung my coat in the gentlemen's cloakroom. The attendant said, 'There are already a few waiting for you. The rest of us will arrive as we come off duty.' The door of the manager's office was open. I went inside. His desk was laid with glasses and drinks – gin, scotch, sherry, bottles and bottles of beer. On a big table were sandwiches, pastries and hors d'oeuvre. Sitting behind the desk was the manager with his secretary on his right. I was astounded when he got up to welcome me, albeit in a very stiff manner.

Trying to sound as friendly as possible, though he had been the cause of my premature dismissal, he said, 'What will you have?'

I knew all who were there so far – Smithy, another usherette, Olive from the chocolate kiosk, Chief, the commissionaire, and his assistant, a little Scots boy.

After ten minutes or so of chatting, eating and drinking, the secretary stood up and said, 'I would like to present you with what we've bought. You said you would like some sheets from us all. We give them to you with our very best wishes for your happiness in retirement.' I got up from my chair and walked over to the desk where the sheets and pillowcases were laid, all wrapped in cellophane with their pink showing through. She presented me with these and an *enormous* sheaf of beautiful, mixed flowers. She went on to thank me for my long and devoted service which she could verify as well as many who were there that night. She said how much I was liked by everyone, and concluded by repeating their best wishes.

This was followed by applause, very loud and very hearty.

I replied simply but without difficulty because, after a few drinks, I can always talk: 'Thank you, my friends, and I realize you are *all* my friends who have so kindly contributed to these lovely presents and attended this very delightful evening that has been prepared for me by the Management. I am most deeply impressed, and would like to thank you all again for your great friendship.'

The manager must have felt a perfect brute.

CHAPTER ELEVEN

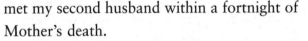

I met my second husband within a fortnight of Mother's death.

I was depressed. I was drinking too much. I went into the Prince of Wales at midday with my Saturday basket of shopping. Maire, a waitress friend, called, 'Hello, Marjorie! You want cheering up!' She insisted on buying me a scotch. A man with a military manner came in and stood at the other end of the counter. Maire looked over and shouted. 'Hello, Jock! Glad to see you!' He came up to us. Maire said, 'This is Jock . . . Marjorie.' I picked up my heavy basket shortly, explaining I was not much company as I'd just lost my mother. He said, 'May I carry that for you?'

At the end of the street, he asked to see me again. I said, 'Oh, you'll see me around.' He said, 'I'm glad. That'll be nice. But can we meet one evening for sure?' I said, 'No, I work in the evenings at the Metropole.' He asked me the time I finished. I told him. 'Right then,' he said. 'Ten o'clock outside the Metropole tonight!'

I was used to men who meet you casually in pubs. He never entered my mind again till I was coming out of the Metropole that Saturday night. 'It's quarter past ten,' I said to myself. 'That fellow at lunchtime said something about meeting him at ten. Anyway, he won't be here.'

I had reached the damp, cold pavement, when someone with a homburg pulled over his face grabbed my arm. He said, 'You didn't think I'd come, did you?'

I let him walk me away like a dog on a lead and found myself drinking with him at the Bag O' Nails. Something just went out to him. There was I, after Mumsie's death, for the first time alone. He came and took her place before I realized the terrible want of her.

His name was Harry Vernon Davison, his regiment the Argyll and Sutherland Highlanders. His favourite animals were monkeys. I called him Monkey First, he called me Monkey Second from the start.

We went to the Dug-Out from the Bag O' Nails. There was no keenness on my part. We had a drink, then he returned home to his digs in Moreton Street. We met again and again. Some nights I let him stay longer.

I can't claim I loved him sexually as I loved Neil Fielding and John Rodger. I wanted him because I was bereft of sex, true. But it was as much a matter of companionship. In life you are given so much love to distribute. When that's gone you have no more love to give. You can only try to care and give some understanding. He seemed to think I was something that had come down from heaven. I said, 'I'll wobble on this pedestal very much, Monkey! Don't put me here! It's very hard to stay up. I'm not like that. You'll find out in time. We all have our faults.' I felt awkward. I felt, 'I can't live up to this. He'll find out that when I drink too much I become obstreperous and nasty. Whisky makes me inclined to wipe the floor with people. I go up in smoke over little things.' He told me I gave him the wish to live. He was so alone. He had nobody to talk to, nobody to love, nobody to do things with. I proposed to him. I asked to take his name and live with him as his wife. Bag and baggage, stamps, medals and skean dhus, he came round to the Dug-Out within the month. He did not deceive me. He put his cards on the table. He warned that he had emphysema, a weak heart and chronic bronchitis and that he might become a burden. He was fifty-six, and he had a wife who wouldn't divorce him. I pooh-poohed the whole thing, arranged at the hospital for a radium insertion, and we went everywhere together as Major and Mrs Davison. Another door had opened as Mother predicted.

I was attracted by his military background. He came off Gallipoli with the Westminster Dragoons at nineteen, and was later promoted to lance-corporal with the Argyll and Sutherlands in Cairo before joining the Military Mounted Police. He attained his majority, still in the East, with the

Sherwood Foresters during World War Two, but had to be invalided out.

After the War, he became a park keeper in St James's. Then the cold mornings got too much for him. When I met him he was a paper keeper at HMSO, Atlantic House. He had an assistant, he told me, to whom he'd shown the ropes. At the end of each day he asked, 'How've you got on?' '*Everything* under control!' was always the reply. Finally Monkey went to check up. He'd never seen such a muddle in his life! For years, '*Everything* under control!' was a joke between us. It meant everything was in a damn bloody mess – the roast burning or me naked when I should have been ready to go out.

He never joined our Metropole group at the Shakespeare. He went to bed at nine. He let me come home as and when I wanted. He could easily have objected, but he never tried to change me. He fell in love with me as I was – bad, good or indifferent.

I made beef or ham sandwiches for him when I got home, and wrapped them in cellophane and put them with an apple in his green zip bag for the office. He'd make tea for us both at six next morning and bring it to the bedroom. I cooked his dinner before leaving for the Metropole. On Sundays he repaid me by doing the roast himself and not letting me near the kitchen. The Bag O' Nails was a regularity beforehand. They used to say at closing time, 'I think we smell your beef roasting!' Occasionally we'd take a taxi to the Queen Mother's church in Pont Street. She, too, is a Presbyterian and a Scot.

He knew all about cooking – a couple of slices of fatty bacon had to go on the roast to give it flavour, and pea rice had only to be par done before going into a chicken. He liked kippers with marmalade and rabbit in cider. He showed me how to cook curry *in* meat by opening the meat up first in a frying pan. He found that salt stops mustard going fusty and that, if Yorkshire pudding has gone soggy and risen round the edges, you can turn it over and it rises the other way.

He wouldn't drink soda with his whisky. He said soda out East really effervesced, you didn't have to turn it upside down before pouring to make it frisky.

I had to show him tolerance. He had a toy monkey called Booboo. Booboo went all through the Second World War with him. She was a part of him. She was sacred. She even had to lie between us in the bed. When I took her to be cleaned he said, 'If she comes back wrong, you may just as well not come back yourself!' Extraordinary in a man of his type! And he wouldn't let me have a cat. He said they were diseased. I said, 'We're *all* disease carriers. A cat might catch a disease from *us*!' He'd have had a monkey, of course, even if it had messed up the whole flat.

He gave me a cuckoo clock. I didn't like it. It was always wrong and it cuckooed at the wrong times. When he wound it I said, 'When the clock stops, the old man dies.'

He wasn't in the least interested in theatricals, and he only liked the old tunes.

Worst of all, he had a bee in his bonnet about Jews. Whenever the word 'Jew' was mentioned, it was like a red rag to a bull. 'Those filthy Jews! I can't bear them!' I tried to calm him. 'You don't know them!' he shouted. 'I've seen them torturing their animals.' I said, 'You might have been born a Jew, and then you would have done the same thing. Anyway, there are good and bad in every crowd.' I gave him lectures. He'd probably have told anyone else to go to hell. Because it was me, he tried to listen. Gradually, whenever I mentioned anything about a Jew – one that I liked or who had done something clever or was musical – he got so that he'd let me talk and never make any remark. There was one thing regarding Jews, though, we *did* agree on, and that was how hard the Nuremberg Trials were on people who had run the camps at pistol point. He made me think that one out.

But the tolerance I showed Monkey was nothing to the tolerance he showed me.

When I cross my legs, I move the top foot up and down. At first Monkey had to shout, 'Stop doing that! It's nerves!' Later, all he had to do was point.

I'm always late. Even in the chorus I used to arrive last tripping over an untied ribbon or with one shoe hanging off. Monkey accepted that. 'Your ten minutes,' he said patiently, 'is what you care to make it.'

I talk too much. Toast burns and milk boils over for my talking. I told him I lost my voice when John was convicted. He laughed. 'Might it ever, do you think, happen again?!'

Then there was the question of my nightmares. I would wake Monkey up with them. I was always running, running towards the edge of a precipice, very, very high up. Someone or something was chasing me. I'd give a piercing scream. Maybe it was all to do with Pearl White films I saw as a child. At the end of an episode she was always left hanging on the edge of cliffs with her figure showing through her draperies.

Worst of all, I drank too much. I still do.

On one occasion, very important to him – it was a dinner of the Argyll and Sutherlands at the Chatham Rooms – I lay flat on the floor, kicking my heels and shouting, 'I'm sick of hearing about these bloody Argyll and Sutherland Highlanders! Take me out of this! Take me bloody home!'

Another evening I went drinking with a mutual man friend in the Strand. Friend! In the early hours Monkey found me on the couch at St George's Drive with my purse open, and one

Guinness bottle open and another missing. 'He could have raped you!' he said. But he knew that wasn't so and that, no matter how drunk, I never would betray his trust.

Chapter Twelve

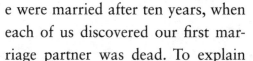

We were married after ten years, when each of us discovered our first marriage partner was dead. To explain the wires and cars arriving and the party downstairs I told Aggie, Indy's successor, who already knew us as Major and Mrs Davison, that we were celebrating an anniversary.

We ordered a taxi to Caxton Hall. I wore virgin white. Monkey was charmed. I thought it rather a comedy after all I'd been through. It also made me look fatter than I need.

The Registrar was delightful. By the end of the ceremony Monkey was almost overcome. Tears were running down his cheeks. I, on my side, wanted to keep things bright and cheerful. I was doing my stuff, putting on my show. 'Thank you,' I said to the Registrar. 'You've made it so beautiful. I *do* hope I'll see you again some time!' All the guests roared, including the Reverend Crow.

Back at St George's Drive we had one round of drinks before the Reverend Crow held a short service from his prayer book. Monkey and I were very moved. Booboo was sat up in a chair. I suppose she was very jealous.

We went off to Brighton on our honeymoon that evening. Brighton was wet, hazy and full of Jews. Monkey hated it. He preferred our usual holidays in Edinburgh and Stirling.

The Argyll and Sutherland depot is in Stirling Castle. The first time we went there we met Colonel Graham. He made a fuss of both of us as I was wearing the Graham kilt and Monkey was one of the few surviving Old Comrades.

The last time we went there, Monkey was an invalid and couldn't make the hill to the Castle on foot. I partly blamed the dampness of the flat. There were slugs that squelched. I was frightened they'd reach the meat safe. I cleared a cupboard. Everything inside it was going mouldy. I took all the cushions one day and put them round the fire. They steamed. We got no heat from the next door basement as that had been condemned.

Aggie, who lived upstairs, was unapproachable. I couldn't like her. Despite a bad hip, she was always coming down to inspect and nose around. One day she called out, 'Mrs Davison, I wish you wouldn't make all those dirty marks on the corridor floor! It's because you take your clothes out to the garden. I'm afraid I can't let you.' I went off the deep end. I said, 'They're not my feet, they're *yours*! Two to three times a week you're running your hose from the bath to the garden! You're far too fussy. To hell with you and your bloody corridor!' I heard Monkey's voice saying, 'Monkey, Monkey! Have you forgotten you're a lady?' I shouted, 'Am I a lady? Am I a bloody lady? I couldn't care less if I'm a whore! She's blaming me for her own footmarks, pretending they're mine!' Then I turned back to her again. I said, 'As far as the bloody line in the back yard is concerned, it's coming down if I never dry another stitch!' She shut up like a clam and went upstairs.

God is just. He has peculiar ways of working. Later her hip got worse and she couldn't come down the stairs at all. She had to have a major operation. The garden has gone to rack and ruin. It's derelict.

Supposed friends of Monkey – an eighty-year-old mother and her daughter of forty – said we could mind a house of theirs indefinitely, seven miles from Liskeard in Cornwall. I packed my old theatrical basket and sent it on ahead.

At Paddington, Monkey was hardly able to get down the platform from the taxi. Our seats were at the far end of the train, and he could only shuffle. He was just about collapsing when a perfect darling of a porter shouted, 'Stand on this, Sir!' and rode him down to our compartment holding on to the side of his trolley.

A car met us at Liskeard. It was a springlike November afternoon. The driver took us quietly. It was the one day Monkey got the lovely fresh air he needed.

The weather got worse and worse from the

moment we arrived, and Monkey couldn't breathe because of the smoke from the damp log fires. I called a doctor. The doctor said, 'I suggest you open the door a little so he has plenty of air as well as warmth.' But that was no good. When I opened the door, the logs smoked more than ever. In the end the doctor was coming once a week.

Some holiday! I was drinking every drop of whisky I could lay my hand on. In the mornings, pouring snow as often as rain, I'd to get dressed in oil-skins, let out the hens and go hewing wood. Then I'd feed the hens and collect their eggs. A big brown one used to come to the front and take all the food. At the beginning I shoo-ed her away. I said, 'Go away, you nasty old thing!' But she wasn't a nasty old thing. We got to like each other. We became such friends she flew onto my shoulder and followed me down and back as I carried the basket I kept in the porch for logs. Three times she layed eggs for me in that basket. I called her Daisy.

After I had cleaned the grates it was lunchtime and I hadn't thought of breakfast. So I just poured myself another fat whisky. Monkey drank, too. A good whack helped him with his phlegm. Something in the spirit tickled his lungs and up it came more easily.

A neighbour drove me to the village every Saturday to buy the week's provisions and collect our pensions.

After Christmas, the old girl came to visit. She had nothing but complaints. I'd given the hens too much grain and hadn't mixed it with enough soft bread. I'd thrown the ashes and cinders on the grass, whereas I should have made a pathway through the wood. I was behind with the fires. 'Do *you* do fires here,' I said, 'or does your daughter? I'm not so much younger than you are, you know!' I spoke to her straight. 'Your wife makes scenes!' she told Monkey.

But for Daisy and a robin I made a pal of, I'd have gone mad. Anyone can have anywhere in Cornwall they like. I wished I'd stayed in town with the damp and the nasty old gas fire that Monkey wasn't supposed to be able to breathe with. Let me say he breathed a lot better with that than he did in the country. I never thought he'd get back to London alive.

What decided me to return was the daughter complaining that I'd stuck up the lavatory. It was one of the sort that run away to a cesspit. Things were appearing in the bath when Monkey and I used it, so I telephoned her. She told me to get a man. I did. He said the pipe hadn't been cleared out in four years. Before giving him the go-ahead, I rang her up again. She asked me what I'd done to choke it. Jokingly, I said, 'I suppose I've been using too much paper!' 'Well, it's funny nothing's ever gone wrong when we were there!' she said. 'You must have been careless!' I said, 'That's what *you* think! Keep your opinion! Blame me for something else in your damned place that I'm hating every minute of! I'll be glad to get out of it! Come back and take over! I'm making arrangements to take Monkey home!' She was a bitch.

So was the mother. When the pair of them arrived to discuss our departure, she said, 'You haven't kept the house very nicely!' I said, 'How *dare* you say that to me! When I came here your furniture hadn't seen a bit of polish for six months, I'm sure!' 'Granted,' she said. 'Well,' I said, 'don't you see it's all been polished now, or has your eyesight gone along with everything else?!' She said, 'I don't remember any chip off the gilt on that picture!' I said, 'You've told me often enough how valuable that picture is! I dusted it most carefully! The chip was already off it!' 'Impossible!!' At which point the daughter had to intervene: 'Mother, that is not so! That chip I did myself.'

They weren't nice people. In March, when we got back to London, I wrote them a letter. I promised that I would never communicate with them again, except at Monkey's dictation. I said our holiday on their farm was a nightmare I intended to forget.

Monkey got so he couldn't dress. He wasn't strong enough to shave. The barber had to call. He had hardening of the arteries. His cough was worse. He was going blind. He had to take all sorts of pills which didn't work. He was under eight stone. He felt the cold even in pyjamas, vest, his thick dressing-gown with a shawl on top, a double blanket round his legs and a hot bottle under his feet. But he said, 'Please don't send me to hospital, dear, as long as you're able to look after me!'

He was rushed to Westminster Hospital one night before Christmas in terrible agony. On Christmas Day my darling was laid there, not well-shaven, ashen, drawn, his dentures out. He was unconscious. I couldn't make him hear. There was a tube in his nose, and a wire coming down – drip, drip, drip – into his arm, which rested on a sort of wooden splint. For two or three hours I held his hand till I realized I was doing him no good and myself no good. At home I drank a bottle of whisky and went to bed.

Next time I saw him, he was bright and sitting up. He said, 'I'm coming home for New Year!' I couldn't believe it. I was thrilled. We had haggis. He was allowed to eat and drink everything he wanted.

But pills and whisky made him temperamental. He was scared of being left alone. He became excited when I told him I'd be out for half an hour and I got back late. Then *I'd* get in a temper. I said, 'Oh, Monkey! For goodness sake! What do you expect when I have to get you your smoked

roe and olives and all the little things you like!'
Then he would weep and say, 'You don't know
how much I love you! You don't love me like I
love you!' Then *I* would weep and say, 'Don't be
so ridiculous!'

Next he began to itch all over. The doctor gave
him special pills, then other pills to counteract
the first pills because they didn't work. Finally he
was sent to the Gordon Hospital in an ambu-
lance for a doctor's examination. He was kept in
for further tests, then returned to me again.

That was the beginning of the end. Though I
had a nurse who called to help me, I couldn't
manage. He wouldn't eat. He collapsed if he tried
to walk. He wouldn't use a bed-bottle. I couldn't
lift him to change the sheets. He'd shout, 'Don't
leave me, Monkey! Don't leave me!'

I found him on the floor one night beside the
bed. At sixty-seven I couldn't lift him on my own.
The doctor insisted he go back to the Gordon
Hospital. 'I'm afraid,' she said, 'he won't be able
to come home to you again.'

Sometimes when I visited him he recognized
me and talked quite sensibly. Once he said,

'Where's home?' Another time he said, 'I'm very tired today. That train journey up to Leicester was too much for me. But maybe I could go to Portsaid tomorrow. I'd really like that!'

One night he fell out of bed and broke his leg. He was operated on at the Westminster, then transferred to the Western General Hospital For Incurables. There were only two beds in his little ward. It was quiet. The walls were made of glass. There were trees round about.

I took him his cards and a bunch of red roses on his birthday. He was seventy-six. His face was rather sunken, but his colour was quite good. He didn't look like a dying man. He was breathing comfortably. A nurse told me she had heard him rambling about a monkey.

Two policemen came to see me next day. With their helmets off, they asked, 'May we come in?' I said, 'I know what it's about. It's about my husband.' They worded it so nicely. They said, 'Yes, he's passed on. Are you all right?'

He was cremated at Streatham Vale. His ashes were strewn in the Garden of Remembrance. He had asked for a St Andrew's flag to cover his coffin, but I could only get a Union Jack. Above it were red roses from his Monkey. The Presbyterian minister came from Stirling, home of the Argyll and Sutherland Highlanders, the regiment of which he was so proud. With me were Frank, a widowed friend and our first footer for many years, and Tom Bachrach, the last Old Comrade of the Westminster Dragoons.

I was alone again, a selfish and spoiled person who had always depended on someone else. Every so often I would remember some remark Monkey used to make and think, 'Oh, never will I hear you say that again!' Tears ran down my face and then, in another minute, it was all over. I was sorry I said what I did about his cuckoo clock, and wound it twice a day myself. I wore his dressing-gown. It was warm and comfy, as if someone put their arms around me and held me tight.

CHAPTER THIRTEEN

You could dress a show with what's in the back room. Even half the bed is heaped with Monkey's clothes – coats, hats, tails, dinner jacket, split-new office wear, socks, his uniform. At first I couldn't attack the idea of sorting without upset. Now I can.

Scotch helps. Monkey called it 'very nice thank you'. I call it medicine. Though we gave in to the fact we spent too much money on drink, we never wasted. We kept the last bottle warming by the fire and bet how many drops would come out of it. Whoever won got the drops. Drink makes me more sociable. It saves me putting on my glasses. It helps me to write a letter and to make decisions. It stirs my imagination. I won't take the pledge. Fear I'll become like my father will have to pull me up instead. I can still say 'No.' I must have *some* will-power because I haven't smoked for twenty-five years – and I smoked twenty Players a day from the age of sixteen. (In the old days you put a shilling for twenty into the machine and got back a halfpenny.) Then Mother said, 'Your chin doesn't stick out enough!', and I took up the challenge.

I have prayed to God – to pray has become more than just the right thing to do; I have prayed for something other than myself to live for, someone to give love to where it's needed. I'm a healthy woman. For two years Monkey couldn't breathe let alone cuddle a huge monster like me.

In Frank I thought my prayer was answered. Almost every day he took me out to lunch or for a drink, and tried to cheer me up. He came with me by taxi to get the Certificate of Death and to the Coroner's Court to get a certificate about Monkey's broken leg.

A week after the funeral he became amorous. I

was his Funny Girl, his Lovey-Dovey. 'Hello, Marjorie!' and a peck on the cheek changed to wanting sexual intercourse. Twice I had to stop him entering the bedroom. Then I changed. I found I had feelings just the same as his. We went to bed together and he couldn't rise to the occasion. Frank was upset. It didn't worry me one scrap. I said, 'Don't blame yourself! I asked you. I wanted you.'

But he didn't speak my language. He wrote to say he was a bundle of nerves, he had seen his doctor, we shouldn't have sex, he had family troubles, he was seventy-three, it was a long way to come . . . I began to be sensitive myself. I wondered did he think I had my claws in him and wanted him to marry me. I explained to him sex wasn't love. From then onwards, everything resumed happily. We met once a week without sex – just a kiss and a hug on arrival and a goodbye kiss and a hug, well meant.

At Christmas he didn't ask me to join him. He sent me flowers and made the excuse he must go to stay with his daughter. And yet he was supposed to love me and he knew I was alone!

I rang him at New Year and invited him to first foot for me. He refused. His daughter was having a party, he said; driving was dangerous when you'd had a drink; the weather . . . That was the weak way out. I pitied him.

I invited a teacher from upstairs to do the honours and, with seven other friends, all kind enough to come and wish me luck as they knew I was living through an unhappy time, I had a marvellous New Year – haggis, bashed neeps, mashed potatoes, fun with a Polaroid camera. I served double-strength whisky in a gravy-boat onto the haggis, ladling it with a toddy spoon. Monkey would have roared! He always said the best of the haggis was the gravy.

I woke in the morning without a headache, right as a trivet and surrounded by empty bottles, dirty glasses, dirty plates. The light was full on and nobody was there but me. I wrote to Frank. When you give love, I said, you don't strew it around like confetti at a wedding.

No reply.

CHAPTER FOURTEEN

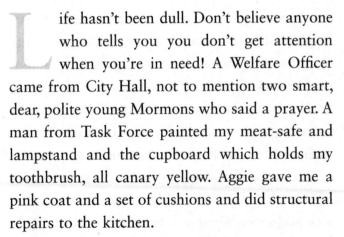

L ife hasn't been dull. Don't believe anyone who tells you you don't get attention when you're in need! A Welfare Officer came from City Hall, not to mention two smart, dear, polite young Mormons who said a prayer. A man from Task Force painted my meat-safe and lampstand and the cupboard which holds my toothbrush, all canary yellow. Aggie gave me a pink coat and a set of cushions and did structural repairs to the kitchen.

For weeks and weeks I filled in papers and answered questions about Monkey's military life. At last, after quite six months, I was awarded more than I ever dreamed of – nearly twelve pounds a week in addition to my Old Age Pension! Also Monkey's £500 Defence Bonds were transferred into my name. I bought a new gas cooker, the latest in gas fires, some kinky boots and a new stretch-cover in kingfisher blue for my Queen Anne chair. I've had a new television set piped in and I take the *Radio* and the *TV Times*, but I do wish before programmes begin they didn't have squares advancing and retreating and dots dotting all over the screen. It tires me out. Why not simply put the title and get on with it?

But best of all, I could afford to redecorate the living room. I spread the word among the builders in Warwick Square, and suddenly, one Sunday at three o'clock, a broad six foot four Scotsman with long ginger hair and a beard knocked at the door and offered to do the job for sixty pounds.

I chose the brightest daffodil yellow, with turquoise relief. Delightful! We drank all the time he was painting. What a life story! A Hebridean Islander, his father a laird, his elder brother a chief, himself a Gaelic speaker and a clansman at Inverness Academy! He sang when he talked. I could have fallen for him. And could he drink! He was always half a bottle ahead – only a spot of water in a large double. No wonder it took him three weeks to do the one room.

The Saturday before he finished, he came back about nine to mend the settee. I seemed sober but I was drunk. I invited him to the Albion round the corner. It was packed. I remember dancing. He said he had to go to meet his wife. I said, 'Why the hell not?! Who's stopping you?!'

I woke up on a mattress in a cell. A police-woman was bending over me, offering me a glass of water and asking did I feel sick. I said Yes to the water and No, I didn't feel the slightest bit sick but where was I? 'Rochester Row Police Station,' she said. 'Was I thrown out of the pub?' I asked. 'I wouldn't know,' she said. 'We picked you up off the pavement in Winchester Street.'

It was four in the morning. Two policemen brought me home in a car with a slip of paper saying I must appear at Bow Street on Monday at ten o'clock sharp.

I spent Sunday sobering up. I had a lightly boiled egg and a cup of tea for lunch, then made myself a roast of lamb and cabbage and roast potatoes. I didn't drink a drop all day. Just television and early to bed. I was so ashamed in one way. In another I could see the funny side. Not everyone gets the chance to have a new experience at my age.

Next morning, with bated breath, I presented myself to a policeman at Bow Street. I apologized for being five minutes late. 'That's all right, Madam!' he laughed, as if to say, 'You must be new here. The Court doesn't start till ten-thirty!'

I was put in a waiting-room with two others – a very young blonde, with hair down to her waist and a skirt up to her navel, and a tatty, down-at-heel old hag muttering something about dry cleaners not returning coats dry. Soon they both went into an adjoining lav and stayed there.

After what seemed a very long time, a policeman came and called out a name. 'Hold on!' yelled the blonde from the lav before appearing and disappearing. In that skimpy skirt of hers, I really thought she'd catch a chill.

Now I began to get collywobbles in the tummy. The hag was back but incapable of conversation. Instead of taking it all as a little joke that was going to interest me, I felt a bit scared and like a child. The policeman called my name. 'Mrs Davison! Come this way, please.' I followed him down the corridor where he parked me at a door in front of a row of six or so peculiar men all leaning against the wall. I was thinking, 'This is like a first night! Here's my entrance!' I was terrified.

I had two minutes in which to get myself worked up, and then the door opened. Well! What an enormous place! On my right, far away, fiddling with things and all dressed up with a hammer to bang, sat the presiding magistrate. On my left were rows of people. I walked along, and up some steps onto a rostrum. Thank God there was a rail! I grabbed hold of it and held damn tight while the charge was made.

There was some discussion. Then the magistrate, after banging his hammer, said in a very distinct and heavy voice, 'Mrs Davison, you were picked up drunk and disorderly near a public house on Saturday night'. (He mentioned the time and place.) 'That is disgraceful behaviour!

Have you anything to say for yourself?' I said, 'No, nothing except sh-shame.' (I was all stuttery). 'I-I-I'm terribly ashamed of the whole thing, and I really didn't understand the seriousness of the charge until this minute.' 'Oh! And how is that?!' 'Well,' I said, 'for a very good reason. This has never happened to me before, and I sincerely hope it will never happen again.'

There was a pause. He'd dried up. I went on. 'All I can say is I'm deeply sorry and terribly, terribly ashamed. I can't even tell you how it happened. All I know is – and I'm telling you the truth – I was in a public house drinking. I certainly had had a lot to drink. I do know that. The next thing I remember is being in Rochester Row Police Station with a very delightful lady policeman asking me was I all right and would I care for a drink of water.' There was dead silence everywhere. He said, 'I hope I have your word, Mrs Davison,' (he addressed me nicely) 'that this will never happen again. It was indeed shameful and I'm very sorry it should have happened to you'. 'Yes,' I said, 'at this late age in life it really is very disgraceful!' I rubbed *that* in. He stared at me. Maybe he didn't think I looked so terribly old. 'Case dismissed!' he said.

I was so relieved that, when I got outside, I thought I'd go and have a drink. Then I checked myself. 'No, that'd be naughty!' Instead I walked in the sun thinking how, to get any idea of what goes on in the world, you've got to go through things and see them for yourself. Reading about life isn't the same.

I went into a restaurant and ordered a cup of coffee and a shrimp and salad roll. Then I walked down the Strand and took a 24 bus home.

Who was busy indoors, but my giant, ginger-bearded Scotsman! I told him what had happened and we celebrated right away.

Drinking gives me happiness. As long as I can afford it I shall carry on. I can fall asleep in the safety of my own home, can't I?

Appendix

9/8/72

Dear Marjorie,

I would be very grateful if you would apply yourself seriously to the book and let me know in due course <u>exactly</u> where the expansions, corrections and insertions and enlivenings are to be made. I feel it would be as unfair to me as to yourself not to do the book to the best of your ability. It would help me considerably if you acted as soon as possible in view of the time I have available for typing. It takes much longer than I believe you realize.

Yours sincerely,
Clive M.

Wed. 9th Aug. 72.

Darling Clive

Well! I just needed your letter to make me realize I must put time and patience into <u>my</u> part at <u>once</u> and apply myself if I want to do anything worthwhile which I <u>do</u> for <u>both</u> our sakes. I need someone to 'bully' me.

My resolution has started and this very 'Highlan' nicht' I promise a <u>beginning</u> and by the week-end I may want to see you for a sherry! Sorry I was a poor hostess the other night but you know you could have opened the sherry yourself! I hope I'll be in your <u>good books</u> the next time I see you. Cheerioh! I'm a busy woman now.

Marjorie

Wed. 16th August '72

Darling Clive

Leave for Edinburgh on day coach <u>8 A.M.</u> <u>Saturday 19th Aug '72.</u> If you can pop in and see me <u>before Saturday</u> I have started work and will take book with me as I may be away two or three weeks and will find plenty of time for writing as

I am not able to rush around as much as I used to do and of course my friends are both out at work all day except week-ends. They have a lovely flat and a garden and the weather forecast is good if that <u>means</u> anything!

Am feeling fit but very pleased to have a change of air. I'm sure I can fill out the book and I promise you I'll do my best. I <u>sits</u> and sometimes thinks!!!

Looking forward to seeing you before I go. Hope you have good news of your lovely mother and also hope you are enjoying your holiday. I have some Harvey's!!! Love Dears!

Marjorie D.

P.S. Excited and busy

Thursday 11.30. 26th Oct 72

Dear Clive,

Letter received. Thanks for those few kind words, I was rather scared until I heard you were pleased with my effort. Think your suggestion of tape again is good. Please <u>anytime</u> after <u>6 o'clock news tonight</u> and again tomorrow morning if suitable. I have made no appointments until next week.

You are marvellous the way you can work. I feel such a lazy bugger. Very cheerful today.

Marjorie D.

Thursday

Dear Clive,

Note received. See you 11 A.M. tomorrow Friday. Will have notes as requested.

Looking forward to a helpful meeting.

Goodnight Clive my good friend and I'm not kiddin.

Marjorie D.

P.S. Hope you are not overworked and tired.

Wednesday 13th Dec.

Darling Clive,

Have managed to get two stalls for Bygraves 18th Mon. Dec. 72. I'm giving them to you in case I lose them.

Keeping fit and loving my new fire. Had some lovely surprise presents and cards already. No word yet from [ ]. I've taken your advice and let sleeping kittens lie in case I write something I might regret. Today is my lovely 13th. and I've been warm and happy indoors, but now must go out for the usual shopping. Am looking forward to the moon walkers again tonight. Hope your cold is now quite gone and you have satisfactory news of your mother.

As always,
Marjorie D.

P.S. Please leave me the book before Xmas. I have decided to write and revise.

2nd Jan. 1973.

Darling Clive

Intended coming up with this early today but did not appear to public eye until 12 – and must have needed sleep badly. Feel wonderful today full of good resolutions like you! Am now putting on paper what I have already promised you. I will start as from <u>tomorrow Wednesday 3rd</u> to do a little to our contribution to world prog-ress!!! It's so dull being too clever – don't you agree! Everyman loves you if you are just too silly. The little parcel of sandwiches are (sic) cer-tainly due to you as you tell me you never found any sandwiches on New Year's Eve. Whenever you feel like it pop down and have a popper with me just we two please. I've one left. Your mother's letter to read also.

   Always affectionately

   Marjorie D.

                       16th Jan. 73.

Darling Clive,

   I cannot believe it's over a week since I've seen you. I've been very busy with book but find I seem to be getting on very slowly <u>although I have worked.</u> New excitement a stalwart highlander. – was sent I'm sure by 'Monkey'. He starts decorating my room next week if I can get it ready. If not, the following week. How very kind of the Moriartys to invite me for <u>Sunday evening 8 p.m.</u> I shall be honoured to accept if you will kindly escort me. Had another nice letter from your mother. She says she is much better in health. I expect you hated work again last week but expect you are getting used to it again by now. I'm so busy I really do not know where to start. Packing and washing bits and pieces. I have such a lot to cope with.

   Happy Days

   Marjorie D.

Tuesday 15th May '73

Darling Clive,

Just to let you know I am still alive and to thank you for your Birthday Wishes. I had a happy and pleasant evening but missed your grunty old face! I planned it all badly so only a few turned up. My friend, Sally, who suffers with arthritis made an effort and came so that was a very happy and pleasant surprise and as you know I like surprises.

I took a package for you <u>by hand</u> last week. Hope you received it safely. If you are not engaged on <u>Sunday next</u> perhaps you could <u>eat with the animal!</u> Make your own time. Just let me know beforehand. Hope you are not over-working. I have got stuck again but still have time to do more for the book before I see you!!! Hope your news is good from your mother. It's awful everywhere else!!!

Love
Marjorie D.

Thursday, 23rd Aug. 73.

Darling Clive,

Book arrived safely. Left on my kitchen window. As usual I must have slept late!

Have read it <u>once</u> and am so excited and thrilled to death with it. You really are a genius and I do so hope for <u>your</u> sake it will sometime repay you for your trouble and kindness to me. Your new approach [ruthless pruning and re-ordering. Ed.] is certainly a wonderful improvement and makes the reading so very much more interesting and there is still a lot of humour as you mention.

Before your return I'll drop you another little line, <u>not</u> another 'epistle to the Corinthians' like the last!!!

I'll re-read and may have some suggestions by then. When I look at that photo I cannot believe I ever looked like that, and really am quite conceited!!!!

I hope you are pleased with your work but a really clever person never is satisfied, am I right?

If nothing ever happens with it I want you to know I will be ever grateful to you for helping me to get over a very difficult time. Even [ ] if he had truly loved me I'm sure would not have made me feel so contented and satisfied and happy with my new life and very firm on my own two feet and so grateful to that <u>someone</u> you know who.

Love again and thanks
Marjorie D.

Sat. 5th Jan. '74

Darling Clive,

What a lovely surprise – your presents and card and thank you – oh! what joy.

I had given you up or rather thought <u>you</u> had given me up and did not blame you – but thought you might have acknowledged the small £5 I sent you with my feeble letter of apology for my behaviour [an amorous advance – Ed.] on the fatal night of the <u>13th</u> Sept. I believe.

Although very very hurt I had begun to think of you as something I had dreamed about that never really existed, someone I had told more to than any living soul. Perhaps I put you in a special class and expected at least understanding.

You ought to know I never pick people, they are sent to me!

I have spent the most unusual Xmas and New Year and at the moment am at the crossroads and do so need some-one to confide in and ask their help. If you feel you can see me again – I still live here and would welcome a visit from you whenever you can spare an evening, anytime next week. Please write and make your own Time and Date.

I know I am 'special' but do not ask VIP treatment.

I do not throw my love away. It usually comes back sometime. I believe I have the last chapters of my life happening now. Perhaps that is why the book is held up!!

Here I am scribbling on so now you know I am still Marjorie or the 'Monkey' who played with fire and at the moment is hellish frightened of everything.

Another extraordinary happening, Clive. The kitten you sent me is here, was given me as a New Year Present. She is called Tibbs and is only six weeks old and a little bitch! She is still very frightened but each day growing more interesting. Please do not disappoint me as I've had a lot of unhappiness during the last few weeks. Again thank you for the lovely presents and wishes.

As always,

Marjorie D.

Sunday 17th Feb. 74.

Thank you my Dear for your delightful card which now has joined the others on my shelf. My first Valentine – and what a thrill! I had begun to think I had lost forever a dear friend, entirely my own fault.

Well! Mr VIP you know you are very welcome and I should love to see you whenever you can spare the time. I have experienced yet something new in my short life!!! [Marjorie had found a man to 'live' with her. Ed.] and would like to tell you all about it, as you alone know more about me than any living soul. Life is very strange, but lovely.

You will be pleased to learn I am <u>off</u> 'whiskey' [sic] and now drink Gordon's Gin and bitter lemon! I feel this is a step in the right direction. Maybe it will be 'the pledge' next. It could happen to me, but not before my 70th birthday DV on the 9th May <u>please.</u> Best wishes and still fingers crossed for the book. <u>Now</u> I <u>do</u> need cash – I'm broke!

Always the 'Monkey'

Marjorie Davison

7th Jan'y 75

Dear 'Clive',

Your cryptic card addressed to my cousin reached me after being twice forwarded.

I am sorry to say that Marjorie Davison died last Spring after a sudden heart attack.

Yours sincerely

–Norman Robertson

17th Nov'r '75

Dear Mr Murphy,

Marjorie died on 22nd March 1974. She had a heart attack on a bus – in Victoria St, I think – and was dead on arrival at Westminster Hospital.

She was undoubtedly a warm and generous person, as you say, and probably at her best when being the life and soul of the party.

Good luck with your efforts.

Sincerely yours

Norman Robertson

P.S. In case it's useful, the Coroner gave cause of death as 'coronary occlusion due to Atheroma' after post mortem without inquest. N.R.

extracts reading groups events
competitions books new
discounts extracts extracts discounts
competitions reading groups extracts
books new extracts discounts events
events books reading groups
extracts new titles reading groups
interviews events new reading groups
events extracts extracts books
discounts new books
new books events interviews new books extracts
events new events interviews new books extracts
discounts extracts discounts books
www.panmacmillan.com
extracts events reading groups books
competitions books extracts new